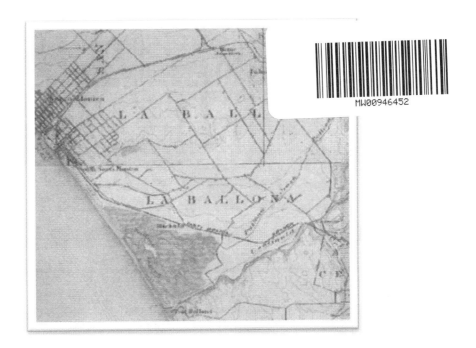

'Round *the* Clump of Willows

The rich history of Westchester/Playa Del Rey,

CALIFORNIA

David J. Dukesherer

'Round *the* Clump of Willows

The rich history of Westchester/Playa Del Rey,

CALIFORNIA

'Round the Clump of Willows

This book is dedicated to My Mother;

Mary Joan Thompson Dukesherer

CENTAL

Dedicated to preserving the memory of
Rancho's La Ballona & Aguaje Centinela

On the Cover; *Islands in the Stream*, "Being against evil doesn't make you good. Tonight I was against it and then I was evil myself. I could feel it coming just like a tide... I just want to destroy them. But when you start taking pleasure in it you are awfully close to the thing you're fighting."

Islands in the Stream, Bimini, Ernest Hemingway

On the Inside Cover; 1902 UNITED STATES GEOLOGICAL SURVEY MAP of Rancho La Ballona, (Courtesy, Wikipedia).

CENTAL Historical Group, Inc.

Los Angeles, California USA

The Cental logo includes the Rancho La Ballona cattle brand

www.rancholaballona.com

Contents

ACKNOWLEDGEMENTS

This volume combines information from my personal writing, photos and vintage postcards, and from many other resources. Much of the information has been drawn from my monthly newspaper column, contained in *The Westchester Hometown News*, Los Angeles, CA, Robin Zacha, Publisher, in issues published between 2002 and 2009, and my columns at examiner.com.

"As you get older, the ground gets harder"

- Richard Farnsworth

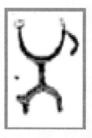

Introduction

A petition was sent to protest the granting of Rancho Ballona to the Machado brothers; Augustin and Ygnacio, and to Felipe Talamantes and his son Tomás. The Ballona grant had belonged to Pío Quinto Zúñiga and his sons but had been rescinded after the death of Pío Quinto because the sons did not comply with the rules governing such grants, such as herding cattle in such a manner that they did not bother the neighboring herds. They lost the grant probably while the elder brother was in the army, about 1808 or 1809. A long list of *vecinos* protesting the re-granting of the *rancho*, which had reverted to public pasture, was added.

Following *regidores* Anastacio Avila and Tomás Uribes, were the names of other persons who presumably had herds in the western coastal area:

Francisco Acebedo, Juan Pollorena,
Máximo Alanís, Ignacio Rendón,
Juan de Dios Ballesteros, Antonio Reyes,
José Bermúdez, Jacinto Reyes,
José A. Botiller, José Antonio Romero,
Ramón Buelna, Mateo Rubio,
José Féliz, Santiago Rubio
Pablo Franco, Vicente Sánchez
Bernardino Higuera, Encarnación Urquídez,
Juan José Higuera, Segundo Valenzuela,
Andrés Ibarra, Cayetano Varelas,
Antonio Ibarra, Mariano Verdugo,
Desiderio Ibarra, Francisco Villa,
José Palomares, Vicente Villa, and José Polanco.

The population had roughly doubled in the Los Angeles district since the death of Zúñiga and there were many more families raising stock in the *pueblo* lands.

A resume of the *ranchos* in the jurisdiction were listed in Goycoachea's memorial of 1802. Rancho Ballona, also known earlier as Los Quintos (from Zúñiga's name, Pío Quinto, which was often used much like a surname in *pueblo* correspondence), was evidently granted shortly after 1802, probably about the same time that the grant of Malibu was made to Bartolo Tapia in 1804.

Correspondence pertaining to the Ballona grant revealed interesting geographical information. Rancho de los Quintos is mentioned as being at the mouth of the Los Angeles River, and it is the one later confirmed as Rancho Ballona. This is a documentation of the tradition that the Los

Angeles River at times changed course and ran out what was later Ballona Creek. According to oral tradition, the river changed course in the flood of 1815, running down the old channel roughly equivalent to Alameda Street and then turning west around the latitude of Exposition Boulevard (the present Martin Luther King Boulevard), down into swamps of La Cienega (Ciénega) and into Ballona Channel.

In the flood of 1825 the river again changed its course, this time again running southward. There has been much debate about this matter, but it would seem that the tradition was accurate. Some earlier accounts of the river's course running down the same westward channel is extant, but the dates are less certain. Perhaps the vagaries of the river may account for the earlier location of the *plaza* being moved in the 1790s, for there seems to be, as mentioned earlier, a more southerly early location on lower ground noted in certain.

The author H.H.Bancroft tells this story of Don Augustin: "The merchant, Don José Antonio Aguirre, owner of the Ship *Joven Guipuzcoana*, once had a new supercargo, who was a stranger to and ignorant of affairs in California.

While the ship lay at San Pedro, Aguirre being absent, Augustin Machado, a well-to-do ranchero, and a man of sterling character, but who could neither read or write, went on board to make purchases, his carretas being at the landing. After selecting his goods, as he was about to place those in a launch to be carried on shore, the supercargo asked him for payment, or some guaranty or note of hand. Machado stared at him in great astonishment; at first he could not comprehend what the man meant.

Such a demand had never been made from him before, nor in fact from any other ranchero. After a while the idea struck him that he was distrusted. Plucking one hair from his beard, he seriously handed it to the supercargo, saying, "Here, deliver this to Señor Aguirre and tell it is a hair from the beard of Augustin Machado. It will cover your responsibility-it is sufficient guaranty." The young man much abashed, took the hair and placed it carefully in his books and Machdo carried away the goods.

Aguirre was chagrined on hearing the story, for Machdo's word was as good as the best bond. José M. Estudillo relates this incident and also the following: In 1850 Aguirre sent Estudillo to Los Angeles to collect old bills, many of which were outlawed; but the greater part of which were finally paid.

He visited Machado's rancho at La Ballona, to collect a balance of about $4000 and happened to arrive when the house was full of company. He was cordially received as a guest and when apprised of the object of his visit, Machado said that he had been for some time thinking that he was indebted to Aguirre, and promised to meet Estudillo in Los Angeles in two days.

At the time appointed Machado was there and delivered the whole sum at the door of Manuel Requena's house, refusing to take a receipt, saying that Aguirre was not in the habit of collecting the same bill twice."

One

Beach of the King

Beach of the King

Rancho Sausal Redondo was a 22,458-acre (91 km^2) land grant given in 1837 to Antonio Ygnacio Avila by Juan Alvarado Governor of Alta California.

The Spanish words, Rancho Sausal Redondo, mean a large circular ranch of pasture with a grove of willows on it. Rancho Sausal Redondo covered the areas that now include Manhattan Beach, Lawndale, Hermosa Beach, Inglewood, Hawthorne, and Redondo Beach, Westchester and Playa Del Rey. (from *Wikipedia*).

After Mexico gained her independence from Spain, the rancho was carved up, creating Rancho's La Ballona and Aguaje Centinela.

The jewel in the crown of the rancho, built in a nest of beach land , and surrounded by the Westchester/Playa Del Rey bluffs and the Ballona Creek; the former course of the Los Angeles River, became Playa Del Rey--Spanish for "beach of the king."

The book covers a period from ancient days through about 1989, and is part one of a two- book project.

Two

How We Got the "D" in Playa Del Rey

A lone 1930's Street Car passes through a lonely Playa Del Rey, California.

The Port Ballona United States Post Office was established in 1889, and after that venture failed, it closed. The town was renamed Playa del Rey in 1902. In 1904, The United States Post Office was established again at Playa del Rey, at the Playa del Rey Pavilion, and dedicated on Thanksgiving Day. Frank Lawton was the first Postmaster.

It was closed in 1914; after the Amusements at Playa del Rey failed. It remained closed for 25 years, and was finally reopened in 1939. In 1924, attempts to rename the town Palisades del Rey, along with parts of southern Venice failed. In 1960, a movement to Anglicize/simplify city names adjusted the proper Spanish spelling of the village, when the name of the town would be changed forever to Playa Del Rey (with a capital D). Result: Playa Del Rey, short for: Playa de el Rey.

In this 1930's photo, the trolley car is passing the old depot on Culver Boulevard, approaching Vista Del Mar. The original Bank of Playa Del Rey building is now a market; advertising Arden Dairies. Arden Farms was started by Edward Robbins in 1904 and was the first certified milk dairy in California.

Arden opened Mayfair Markets, and eventually Gelson's Markets.

PLAYA DEL REY LAGOON, PAVILLION AND HOTEL, 1905. This post-card view of the Lagoon development, is probably the most replicated view of Playa del Rey; the former and failed development of Port Ballona. It is taken from atop Mount Ballona; now Montreal Street, looking down on present day Culver Boulevard.

Three

Westchester/Playa Del Rey Holidays; Our Spanish heritage

The Holidays have again spirited up on me, and again we will celebrate Christmas Eve with Spanish and Mexican food, reminding us of and in homage to our rich local heritage. Although I am German/Irish/French, I lived for awhile on another old Spanish possession; the archipelago of Puerto Rico and you have not lived until you have spent a holiday season with parranda's and asaltars. In 1493, Columbus named the island San Juan Bautista, in honor of Saint John the Baptist (second cousin of Jesus), but it was later renamed; "Rich Port".

In Westchester and Playa Del Rey, it is very hard to escape that heritage; with many streets, towns and attractions named or derived from old Spanish history.

La Tierja; "the scissors", intersects **La Cienega** at out eastern border. The Spanish phrase la ciénaga translates into English as "the swamp" and the area named "Las Ciénegas" was a continual marshland due to the course of the Los Angeles River (Ballona Creek), through that area prior to a massive southerly shift in 1825 to roughly its present course. The difference in spelling between the Spanish word ciénaga and the name of the thoroughfare originated with the name of the rancho.

Sepulveda Boulevard, which stretches some 42.8 miles from Rinaldi Street at the north end of the San Fernando Valley to the city limits of Hermosa,(beautiful), Beach, where it "jumps" 1.3 miles east and continues on to Long Beach. It generally runs north-south, passing underneath two of the runways of Los Angeles International Airport (LAX). It is the longest street in the city and county of Los Angeles. Sepulveda Boulevard is named for the Sepulveda family of San Pedro, California. The termination of Sepulveda is on a part of the Sepulveda family ranch, Rancho Palos Verdes, which consisted of 31,619 acres of the Palos Verdes Peninsula. The original grantee of the King of Spain was Jose Dolores Sepulveda. When he was killed in an Indian uprising just above Santa Barbara in 1824, the rancho went to his oldest son, Juan Capistrano Sepulveda.

Sepulveda, and for that matter Lincoln Boulevard, are often confused as being part of the famous El Camino Real. The history of El Camino Real and its' bells is quite interesting. At the same time that the American colonies were rebelling against England, a handful of Spaniards and Mexicans established outposts up the California coast. The first was established in 1769 at San Diego, when they established a fortress and a Franciscan mission. A footpath, called The El Camino Real, or Kings Highway, was created to connect the missions. However, is it highly unlikely that any of the road passed through Westchester.

View of the adobe at Rancho Aguaje de la Centinela, Westchester, 1930. The adobe was originally owned by Ignacio Machado, and the rancho's title translates into "Watering place of the Sentinel". The Bells of the El Camino Real, right, are a modern initiative developed by California Federation of Women's Clubs in 1902. (Complements, Google Books).

Loyola Boulevard, paved before even Manchester Boulevard was developed, opened the area to the new University around 1929. The colleges namesake; Saint Ignatius of Loyola, (1491– July 31, 1556) was a Basque-Spanish knight, who became a hermit and priest, founding the Society of Jesus and becoming its first Superior General.

Centinela Boulevard; "the sentinel," Redondo; "Rancho Sausal Redondo; Ranch of the Round Clump of Willows," and of course Playa Del Rey; "Beach of the King", all owe their names to the Spanish language. On old maps the cliffs of Ballona's easterly boundary are labeled "Guacho," sometimes "Huacho," an Indian term meaning high place; where Westchester and parts of Playa Del Rey are today.

All over the area, and throughout the State, the Roman Catholic Saints (San or Santa), are well remembered; Monica, Gabriel, Francisco, Fernando, Maria, Barbara, Catalina and Clemente, Jacinto, Diego and Jose. San Diego is a Spanish male name derived the Hebrew for Jacob, via the name of Saint James the Great (Sant Yago), re-analyzed as Santiago and San Diego. The assimilation of the final "T" of Sant into the name, a process called sandhi, has also occurred in "Telmo", the Spanish and Portuguese name for Elmo. How does that tickle you?

Christmas, 1960. About 10 years before and before Visitation Church Westchester was built, Christmas Mass was said in our Great-Aunt Martha's garage. The elder members of my family were born in a house just a few doors from the Centinela Adobe. (Juan, Tomas, Daniel, Cristina, David and Kevin).

In 1842, six years before the better-publicized discovery in the **Sacramento** area, Francisco Lopez made the first documented discovery of gold in California (the document is a mining claim signed by Gov. Juan B. Alvarado in that year). The discovery was made in **Placerita Canyon**, an area later used as Hollywood's original back lot. We call the area today; **Santa Clarita**.

Speaking of **Sacramento**; our State Capital, the city is actually named for the Blessed Eucharist. In 1799, Spaniards were so overwhelmed by the beauty and richness of the valley, they exclaimed; *Es como el sagrado sacramento!;* "This is like the Holy Eucharist!" And so they named the town.

So whether you hanker for *tapas or tamales,* Sangria from your *botas,* Sherry *(Jerez)*, or a nice *Cava,* enjoy the Holidays. Enjoying your family and friends, and the age old traditions that bind us together, is what the Holidays are all about. Oh; and blue shirts.

And, we should all be mindful of Luke, 2:9-14; because it all began here;

And, lo, the angel of the Lord came upon them, and the glory of the Lord shone round about them: and they were sore afraid. And the angel said unto them, Fear not: for, behold, I bring you good tidings of great joy, which shall be to all people. For unto you is born this day in the city of David a Savior, which is Christ the Lord. And this shall be a sign unto you; Ye shall find the babe wrapped in swaddling clothes, lying in a manger. And suddenly there was with the angel a multitude of the heavenly host praising God, and saying, Glory to God in the highest, and on earth peace, good will toward men.

Have a very Happy Thanksgiving and Christmas; Felicidades, and Feliz Navidad!

Four

Further Development at Playa Del Rey: An Open Letter

October 22, 2009

Los Angeles Councilman Bill Rosendahl
City of Los Angeles, Council District 11
7166 W. Manchester Boulevard
Westchester, CA 90045

Dear Bill,

I would like to tell you a story. All good stories begin with; "Once Upon a Time," and have a happy ending, and I hope that this one does.

Once Upon A Time, in a place called Playa Del Rey, California; formerly known as Port Ballona, California, a group of visionaries created the new town. Great men, with names like Sherman, Trask, Gillis, Clark and Rindge, they carved out a settlement that was then considered a worthless slough. Earlier attempts to develop a deep water port at what is now Del Rey Lagoon, had failed when the promoter Moses Wicks lost the battle to the interests of the late Phineas Banning.

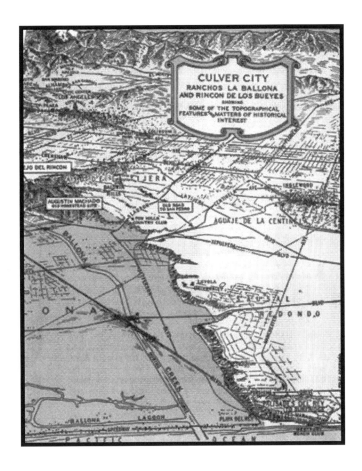

A grand resort was established on the Lagoon. The Los Angeles Pacific "Red Cars" serviced the area and a school, library, post office and bank were established at this new hamlet. Thousands of people came to Playa Del Rey to visit the Amusements and stayed at one of the two hotels. But time and tastes changed, and by the beginning of World War I, the area was near desolate. What the economy hadn't ruined, storms finished off, and again the area became a footnote on most maps of the day.

Fortunately for this story, and the town, along game another great man, Fritz B. Burns, who with the tenacity and perseverance of ten men, created a *new* Playa Del Rey, and in doing so developed Palisades Del Rey, Olympic Beach (now called "Toes Beach), Del Rey Hills and Surfridge. The town he developed had lost its Post Office, and the bank would become one of the first Co-Operative Grocery Stores in the area. Farmers who grew on fields along Manchester and Jefferson Boulevards, would trade their crops of celery, cauliflower and Lima beans, for canned goods and other staples. Cash was tight in those days and barter was commonplace.

Fritz Burns, of the real estate firm of Dickinson and Gillespie, maintained an office where Tanner's Coffee is located today, and served free lunches to prospective clients at about where Outlaw's Restaurant is located.

Del Rey Lagoon, 1901.

Only a few years later: about 1908, the village of Playa Del Rey was a bustling amusement area. The building to the lower right is the first bank in Playa Del Rey, built about 1903.

But even Fritz Burns, who had built an enormous mansion at Palisades Del Rey, could not fight the Great Depression, and in 1930 lost it all. His Waterloo Street mansion(later renamed Waterview), was foreclosed on, and he was reduced to living in a tent, located just about where the Cafe Pinguini sits today; where Culver Boulevard kisses the sweet sand dunes of Toe's Beach.

But as I said, Fritz Burns was no ordinary man, and as the United States economy recovered, so did Mr. Burns, and as a result, we probably owe to Fritz Burns, more than any other man, the legacy which is now Playa Del Rey.

In the end, the wonderful; beachside community of Surfridge, would fall prey to eminent domain, and was wiped out by LAX expansion. The southern section of Palisades Del Rey was lost too, along with a swath of land extending all the way through Del Rey Hills to and through its younger cousin; now called the Town of Westchester. Something like 10,000 homes went under the wrecking ball.

Just north, the largest man-made pleasure harbor in the world would be built along the former estuary of the Los Angeles River; Marina Del Rey was born.

Dickinson and Gillespie Operation, 1921. The Bank of Playa Del Rey is just out of the picture to the right, on Culver Boulevard at present day 179/181 Culver Boulevard.

Nevertheless, what were left were two fine communities; Playa Del Rey and Westchester, California, and for twenty years or so the great towns re-established themselves yet again. These towns were intersected by one of the last great California Wetlands area, where threatened species fought for a toe hold against Man, pollution and further development. And what was once one of the great surfing spots in Southern California, breakwaters and noise pollution reduced it to empty beaches and altered swells.

Villains come and villains go in any story, but in the end, and despite further development at Playa Vista, California, the village of Playa Del Rey remains. Like many places in the world, its' residents love living here, and although many recognize areas where things could improve, most residents agree that further development or "densification" would have catastrophic consequences. Already, the main thoroughfare, Culver Boulevard, formerly called Speedway Boulevard, has become a "commuter freeway" for folks fighting their way out of and back into the southern beach communities. Residents have witnessed; speeds in excess of eighty miles an hour, thirty minute traffic jams and several deaths have occurred on the strip as a result.

You might remember the speech that came from a movie called Network-1976:

Howard Beale:

I don't have to tell you things are bad. Everybody knows things are bad. It's a depression. Everybody's out of work or scared of losing their job. The dollar buys a nickel's worth; banks are going bust; shopkeepers keep a gun under the counter; punks are running wild in the street, and there's nobody anywhere who seems to know what to do, and there's no end to it.
We know the air is unfit to breathe and our food is unfit to eat. And we sit watching our TVs while some local newscaster tells us that today we had fifteen homicides and sixty-three violent crimes, as if that's the way it's supposed to be!
We all know things are bad - worse than bad - they're crazy.
It's like everything everywhere is going crazy, so we don't go out any more. We sit in the house, and slowly the world we're living in is getting smaller, and all we say is, "Please, at least leave us alone in our living rooms. Let me have my toaster and my TV and my steel-belted radials, and I won't say anything. Just leave us alone."
Well, I'm not going to leave you alone.
I want you to get mad!
I don't want you to protest. I don't want you to riot. I don't want you to write to your Congressman, because I wouldn't know what to tell you to write. I don't know what to do about the depression and the inflation and the Russians and the crime in the street.
All I know is that first, you've got to get mad.
You've gotta say, "I'm a human being, god_____! My life has value!"
So, I want you to get up now. I want all of you to get up out of your chairs. I want you to get up right now and go to the window, open it, and stick your head out and yell:
I'm mad as hell, and I'm not going to take this anymore!"

But Bill, I think I got off point; but I am, and many others are, MAD AS HELL. We are mad because new developers are trying to build on those precious dunes, and along the Lagoon and around the landmarks of the Dickinson and Gillespie Building and the Bank of Playa Del Rey and all over the place!

Bill, you might be our last hope. You have to stop the madness and listen to your constituents and open a window and shout; THE BUCK STOPS WITH BILL! We need to look at logical ways to preserve what is left, and stop paving over what is there. We need to find ways to control the traffic and beautify the Boulevard and find other ways to get folks to stop and stay awhile, not just run through town at fifty miles an hour!

Christian Nestell Boyee wrote; *"The grandest of all laws is the law of progressive development. Under it, in the wide sweep of things, men grow wiser as they grow older, and societies better"*.

Have we grown wiser? When does progressive development spell destruction?

Bill, Playa Del Rey needs another great man now; it could be you.

Let's make the end to this story a Happy One.

Thank you,

Five

History is made again... in Westchester as Kohl's Department Store opens

With **Mervyn's** Dept. Store closing, and **Kohl's** <u>now open</u>, they have stepped into a building with tremendous historical heritage.

The current location of the now defunct Mervyn's opened as a department store with great fanfare in 1949, as **Milliron's Department Store**. Just a few years later, Milliron's- Westchester was acquired by **Broadway Stores**, and The Broadway-Westchester operated here for decades. Many locals will remember the roof-top parking, and Rooftop Garden Restaurant, that was a famous place for mothers to take their daughter to tea. It was without argument the anchor-store of the then vibrant shopping center for all of Playa Del Rey and Westchester. The Broadway was a department store chain founded in 1896 by English-born Arthur Letts, and was one of the dominant department stores in Southern California. In 1996 the chain was acquired by Federated Department Stores, and for a brief time operated a **Macy's** store at this address.

MILLIRON'S DEPARTMENT STORE, GRAND OPENING, 1949. 1949 LA Herald Examiner: "Exterior view of the new modern Milliron's store in Westchester. The unique display houses are set at an angle for the benefit of auto traffic on Sepulveda Boulevard. Exterior view of the new Milliron's store in Westchester on March 17, 1949. A large crowd was drawn to official opening ceremonies at the store on Sepulveda Boulevard near Manchester." (PHOTO, courtesy Los Angeles Public Library).

The former Milliron's location traces its roots to one of the most prolific architects in history; sometimes credited with "inventing," and called the Father of the shopping mall: immigrant Victor Gruen.

Gruen escaped Nazi occupied Austria in 1938, and eventually came to California with his new wife, and co-worker, Elsie Krummeck. They eventually designed the location, and began a lifelong successful career in designing shopping centers. This building was his first major project. Many new innovations were created here, including the angled display houses; angled so that passing cars could see the clothing and other goods on display.

MILLIRONS DEPARTMENT STORE, (1949). It was in this display house that the Westchester Santa Claus would greet kids each Christmas season.

(PHOTO, courtesy Los Angeles Public Library).

The display houses and many of the display windows are long gone, as is access to rooftop parking and restaurant. Old time residents will remember that The Broadway sponsored a window painting competition every Halloween. Teens would paint huge mural-like paintings on the windows, and awards were given to the goulie-spooky artists. When I was a kid, it was great fun walking along Sepulveda Boulevard viewing the art.

Also when I was a kid, this part of Westchester was a vibrant, meaningful part of the town; much more so than today, although many recent improvements have brought the vital shoppers back to the Boulevard, we still have a long way to go. Years ago, neighborhood residents had the luxury of two department stores, The Broadway and JC Penney; two theaters, Thom McCann Shoes, See's Candies, Monroe's Men's Store, Woolworth, Newberry's, Thrifty's, and specialty shops such as jewelry and pet stores—and many more. Wasn't it great to get lemonade or an ice cream sundae at the lunch counters? And the whole place was as safe and friendly as your Mom's kitchen. Whatever happened to places like Hy Green's Sports Den?

I am not an expert in this sort of thing, but I too believe that the department store is the key to "anchor" the town, and draw in the shoppers to the area. Moreover, to keep residents, including the students of LMU and Otis Colleges, trading locally, and creating jobs for locals in the process. By the way, there is a second story at the Mervyn's, or at least there was, and perhaps the rooftop parking could be restored.

MILLIRON"S, 1949. Here is an aerial shot of the location and roof top parking and restaurant. The vacant lot, top right, is where Trader Joe's and Spring Cleaners, etc, are located.(PHOTO, LAPL).

UPPER LEVEL PARKING. This is a view of the entrance to the rooftop parking lot, later closed as you can see from the photo on the right. This is at the south side of the building on La Tierja.(PHOTOS, Google).

GRUEN AND KRUMMECK, graffiti painted, commemorative plaque. As the end of the war approached, Gruen became more and more interested in the concept of shopping centers as the ultimate retail achievement. As with his other retail endeavors, Gruen sought to combine the concepts of a retail shopping facility with a social and entertainment center. (PHOTOS, Google).

Gruen believed that the shopping center was the heart of any community, and without one, a town would eventually grow stagnant. We have a chance to rally around this grand old dame, and make sure that developers continue to try and do the right thing in Uptown Westchester.

And here is a little trivia. When Milliron's opened, the door handles were shaped like an "M," and the Broadway turned them upside down creating a "W", signifying "Westchester." Mervyn's cleverly turned them back so that they would spell "M" for Mervyn's.

I hope that Kohl's knows this, and turns them back around, to signify: **Kohl's Westchester**

Six

A New City: Westchester/Playa Del Rey, California

Every so often, when the kettle of frustration reaches a boil and threatens to blow the top off, the issue of the secession of Westchester and Playa Del Rey from the City of Los Angeles resurfaces.

We look around at the cities of Manhattan Beach, El Segundo, Culver City, Hermosa Beach, Santa Monica, etc., and wonder if we were given the control to govern our area, *sans* the ineffective and unresponsive control of the clearly inept City system, would we be left with a better place. The fact is that for many years; over a century in fact, the folks involved in this movement tried to accomplish things by working with City Hall, but the system is so bureaucratic that it is simply impossible.

According to School of Public Policy professor Eric H. Monkkonen, an expert in the historical development of cities and municipal fiscal policy, L.A.'s breakup into smaller entities would have mixed results.

"Big cities have more clout in certain respects, such as securing an Olympic Games," Monkkonen said. "But they also tend to be less efficient."

And if the state of the Westchester school system is any barometer of inefficiency: producing poor-lackluster results, it is time to turn the heat up. After all, how much worse could it get?

Just for a moment, think what we would end up with if we were successful in creating a new city (in no particular order):

1. LAX, the counties second busiest airport, and the fifth busiest worldwide, and an airport we

could start to work with to develop resident friendly solutions with, and if the management there didn't get in line, we could simply fire them. Imagine that?

2. Massive utilities such as the Los Angeles Hyperion Works, the Scattergood Power Generating Station, and the Gas Company; all of which fall within our borders,

3. A wonderful downtown shopping district which we could re-mold into the central-focus of our town, which of course it was intended to be, and not some place where most of the fearful merchants cannot have public doors facing Sepulveda Boulevard, for fear of bums or criminals terrorizing their establishments,

4. Elementary, middle and high schools which we could work towards rehabilitating, and returning to a place of academic prominence,

5. Hotels, a large town park, a lagoon and wet-lands, two state-of-the-art fire stations, several world class universities or satellite universities, and all the rest of the infrastructure a community needs,

6. Dockweiler Beach; need I say more?

And what do we lose? Not much, and whatever we would lose could be replaced with more affordable solutions. And solutions that address the needs of local residents, and not those of greedy developers and interlopers who have little or no stake in the destiny of our town.

We have come a long way, and we created the Department of Neighborhood Empowerment, which allows communities to form their own councils with the power to make recommendations to the city council. But, and I will admit I am no expert, our council has little positive effect on the state of the regions educational system. I am not shooting any arrows at anyone, just stating the facts as they are pointed out on this website.

Professor Monkkonen, went on to say, "All people have to do is look around and see the performance of smaller cities. They haven't sunk, and it's clear to most that these city governments satisfy their residents."

"Much of what big cities do is small potato stuff, like filling potholes, which can be handled just as easily by a small city. Then again, large cities have the revenue to afford things like special police investigation units," he added.

Of course, we have a police department from which to launch these initiatives from: The LAX Police Force, which we could adopt as our new primary law enforcement agency. I certainly have not heard many complaints about other local P.D.'s: such as those at El Segundo and Manhattan Beach. In fact, I have heard nothing but praise from local residents.

And how do we pay for this new City? I have that all figured out. Since we have for years been a town that has mostly been identified as the location of LAX, effective immediately, each and every vehicle that enters the airport will pay a toll of $1.00. Since we have lost a great part of our town to the development of LAX, we will now accept this fee as partial payment for the land we lost, and for the inconvenience of dealing with the ever increasing traffic congestion, noise and air pollution.
Finally, we need to devise a new fee for the task of processing the waste of the City of Los Angeles.

Since we would "control" the Hyperion we would charge for all the waste that we have to process and all the other flotsam and defecation that we seem to be burdened with: which in my mind, we certainly never asked for nor do we deserve, but one way or another ends up in Westchester/Playa Del Rey.

This may all seem like baloney to some, but try to remember that once upon a time this was an area known as Rancho la Ballona; and maybe one day it could be again.

Seven

Once Upon A Time; The NOT So Wide Beaches Of Playa Del Rey

We take for granted the wide sandy beaches at Dockweiler Beach, but it wasn't always the case. Historically in fact, it is a new situation, and you might be surprised to learn, it is man-made.

When the beach areas of Playa Del Rey; Palisades Del Rey and Surfridge were first developed, the sandy beaches were just a few yards wide. If you take into account that the majority of that coastline; just below the bluffs and Vista Del Mar Coast Highway, was graded to handle the trolley-car tracks that ran along the coast as far south as Redondo Beach, in some cases the usable sandy beach was only a few feet wide.

Los Angeles "Red-Car" tracks heading south at Surfridge, Playa Del Rey; about 1921. (Complements, Los Angeles Public Library).

In the 1920's, tons of sand was dredged near Imperial Highway and Vista Del Mar when the Los Angeles Hyperion was expanded. Then in the 1960's, the area known today as Marina Del Rey was excavated. It was the sand from these two projects; deposited at Dockweiler Beach, which created the wide sweeping sandy beaches that we enjoy today.

Eight

Moses Sherman led the people to the promised land; but he was no General

"GENERAL" MOSES HAZELTINE SHERMAN, 1853-1932. (Complements Los Angeles Public Library).

Vermont born Sherman moved to Arizona as a schoolteacher but soon began his long career in banking, land speculation and the development of transportation systems. After running a canal project in Arizona, he moved to Los Angeles in 1889.

Despite a long history of bank fraud scandals and conflicts of interests, he along with his brother-in-law Eli Clark, began to buy up horse-drawn rail -lines and converting them to electric power.; founding the Los Angeles Consolidated Electric Railway Company. His Playa del Rey lines were eventually acquired by Henry Huntington of the Southern Pacific, and serviced the area purchased by the Beach Land Company; the former Port Ballona, which he was of course a stockholder in.

He was never a General of the Army, and bestowed that title on himself; creating an interesting and timely confusion between himself and the great Civil War hero General William Tecumseh Sherman.

In 1902 he was appointed to the first Los Angeles Water Commission. He later went on to develop the town of Sherman; now West Hollywood, California, and much of the San Fernando Valley, which was made habitable when the First Los Angeles Aqueduct was started at Owens Valley in 1905. Sherman Oaks is named for him.

Sherman's "Red Cars" made it possible for early Angeleno's to discover the Westside.

Nine

LAX Ghost Town: Surfridge, Playa Del Rey, California

Travelers need not travel to the California desert or abandoned silver and gold mines of the Eastern Sierra to explore ghost towns, as Playa Del Rey boasts its own specter neighborhood-Surfridge, Playa Del Rey, CA. Once an idyllic beachside community, comprised of over 800 homes on 470 acres, all that is left are the abandoned roads and a few walls and fences.

Streets like: Ivalee, Jacqueline, Napoleon, Waterview, Rindge and Kilgore are there-but the homes are gone, having fallen prey in the late 60's and early 70's to four forced rounds of condemnations by the City of Los Angeles and LAX. Close to 70% of the tab was picked up by the Federal government. Sandpiper (known to many locals as "Thrill Hill,") remains the only open street through the location, although barricaded, temporarily I hope, since "9-11."

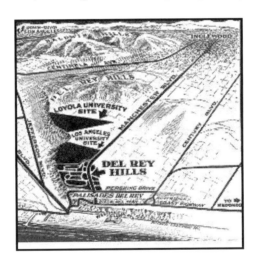

Surfridge became- eminent domain, on grounds of health and safety hazards and gross zoning violations-aka/ "jet noise." Property owners were forced to move, receiving only a fraction of what their homes would be worth today, and creating one of the most expensive pieces of barren land on the planet-wiping the town off the face of the map. The price for paid for Surfridge? $60 Million dollars or about $125,000.00 an acre! Although 66% of residents voted to sell, many still feel that they were forced to sell, as the airport had already destroyed their properties. Those that did not sell saw their homes condemned, and in a few cases, were forcibly removed from their own land. Many of the homes were custom built beach homes and cottages, owned by movie stars and luminaries of the time, including MGM Pictures mogul and Academy Award nominated director Cecil B. Demille. The streets were originally part of a 1921 Dickinson & Gillespie Co. development called "Palisades Del Rey", billed as "The Last of the Beaches". The sidewalks were laid in 1932, by J. L. McClain, Contractors.

After the beach-side homes were bought and/or removed, airport officials began to discuss alternative uses for the property, including a new 18 hole "Pebble Beach" style golf course, a 12-acre sand dune park, and a butterfly reserve.

The California Coastal Commission squashed the golf course and the park, so in the end, it was the butterflies that won the battle-the El Segundo blue butterfly-left to flutter the eerie-foggy dunes and cracked- weed filled streets and foundations- along with the ghosts of Surfridge, California.

Ten

Historic Playa Del Rey corner might be affected by new development

PLAYA DEL REY RED CARS; ON THE PIER, OFF THE DEL REY LAGOON, 1906.

Electric trolleys first traveled in Los Angeles in 1887.

The Pasadena and Pacific Railway was an 1895 merger between the Pasadena and Los Angeles Ry and the Los Angeles Pacific Ry (to Santa Monica.) The Pasadena and Pacific boosted Southern California tourism by living up to its motto "from the mountains to the sea."

And the "sea" in those days spelled Playa del Rey. After many mergers, the area would be serviced by the famous Pacific Electric "Red Cars."

At what is now the intersection of Vista Del Mar, Culver Boulevard and South Vista Del Mar Lane, sits one of the most historic buildings in the area; the former headquarters of

Fritz Burns at Dickinson and Gillespie Real Estate. Recently, this building achieved historic landmark status.

Of equal interest, and just across the street sits the location of the first bank in Playa Del Rey at 179 Culver Boulevard, just next door to the world famous hamburger eatery; The Shack.

FIRST BANK IN PLAYA DEL REY LOCATION, REAR VIEW, CIRCA 1981.

It you head up Culver Boulevard a few yards to Matilla's Del Rey Plaza's parking lot, then you will be at the location of the Los Angeles Pacific Electric Playa Del Rey Station.

Playa Del Rey "Red Car" Station, circa 1920.

1938 view of The Village at Playa Del Rey. The two story structure in the lower center of the photo is the first bank in Playa Del Rey, which opened about 1903. To the right of the bank is the Dickinson and Gillespie Building; and across the street, the trolley station.

Today, Culver Boulevard, not so affectionately known by residents as : The Manhattan Beach Freeway, is inundated daily with thousands of cars that use the route through the town for their commute, despite the fact that Imperial, the 105 Freeway, and Westchester Parkway were designed specifically for this use.

INTERSECTION OF VISTA DEL MAR AND CULVER BOULEVARD, FORMER LOCATION OF THE LOS ANGELES PACIFIC RED CAR STATION-PLAY DEL REY

Finally, and to make matters worse, several developers are trying to "densify" parts of the town with new high density apartments and condos.

When will it all end?

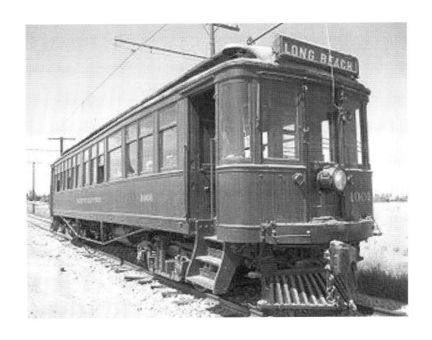

Los Angeles Pacific Electric Red Cars ran from downtown Los Angeles to Playa Del Rey until the 1950's.

Eleven

Early Frenchmen of Los Angeles and Playa Del Rey

Indeed Playa Del Rey and Westchester, and for that matter all of Los Angeles, can boast a long and proud French heritage. Les acclamations au français don't je l'un suis !

French influence in Los Angeles began even before the city itself was founded. It was actually Théodore De Croix (b. Lille 1730 - d. Madrid 1791), ruler of the Northwestern Provinces of Mexico for King Charles III of Spain, who recommended the founding of a pueblo on the banks of the Porciúncula. This wish was realized by Governor Felipe de Neve who signed the proclamation of foundation on August 26, 1781. On September 4, 1781, "El Pueblo de Nuestra Señora la Reina de Los Angeles" was inaugurated.

It was then necessary to wait until Mexican independence in 1822 for California to be open to non-Spanish immigrants. The establishment of the Spanish Basques explains, for the most part, the large attraction of their cousins from the Soule, Basse-Navarre, and Labourd regions to California.

The Basques maintain to this day a great tradition of cattle breeding and farming in Southern California, and maintained large herds beneath the Bluffs of Westchester. The first French immigrants, former members of Napoléon Bonaparte's old guard who had fought for Mexican independence from Spain, arrived in the Pueblo around 1828 with their leading officer Louis Bauchet.

In 1860, 600 of the estimated 5000 inhabitants of Los Angeles were either French or spoke French. Not only did 1859 have one of the highest rates of French immigration to Los Angeles, but it also signaled the importance of the French Colony in civil matters with the election of Damien Marchessault as Mayor. He would be reelected many times. In 1865-66, it was another Frenchman, Joseph Mascarel, who was elected mayor of Los Angeles. It is particularly significant to note that Angelinos elected Frenchmen to serve as Mayor of Los Angeles during the entire period of the American Civil War.

Marchessault and his partner Victor Beaudry (a French-Canadian), were ice vendors, and helped to found an area near City Hall called Frenchtown. At first, they sold ice blocks to saloon keepers. But after building their ice house in 1859, they sold ice door to door throughout the summer months. Marchessault also built the first water distributing system with Charles Lepaon in 1863. Marchessault's success in these activities certainly kept him in contact with a large part of the population.

This was also the case of numerous other Frenchmen, including his nephew Jean Trudel, who supplied the city with salt reclaimed from Playa del Rey.

Playa Del Rey's first operating business: Jean Trudel's salt works was located near present day Del Rey lagoon. Remnants of the salt house were still visible well into the 1900's. PHOTO: Del Rey Lagoon, 1902.

Also in this period, an Alsatian by the name of André Briswalter pursued farming and sold his vegetables door to door with a horse and wagon. The growth and success of his business allowed him to purchase vast tracts of land, including much of what is today known as Playa Del Rey. At his death, he left $25,000 for the building of a church over his tomb (St. Peters Church at 1039 North Broadway).

French restaurants had been an integral part of our city since the dusty pueblo days of the Old West, but except for Taix French Restaurant and Philippe's; the French dip sandwich place, both of which have left their original Frenchtown locations, our choices are few.

Twelve

Don Mateo Keller: the Prince of Malibu

Early Southern California was organized by a small group of amazing men and women. Men like Banning, Huntington and Don Benito Wilson. However no story about pre and post Mexican Southern California would be complete without mentioning Mathew "Don Mateo" Keller.(note: several spellings of his name have been used: Mathew or Matthew/Mateo or Matteo).

I was fortunate enough to attend high school with the great-great grandson of Don Mateo. His name is Tom Cleary and we have been collaborating on a biography of Keller.

DON MATEO KELLER.

In the early 1860's, the Malibu grant passed through the tax sale into the hands of Mathew Keller, better known in those days as "Don Mateo." His cost was about .10 an acre. But the title was disputed, and it took many years for the matter to be resolved.

In 1870 a survey of the land was made by the United States Surveyor General. The map was approved and on August 19, 1872, President Ulysses S. Grant did "give and grant" the Rancho Topanga Malibu Sequit to Keller. Henceforward, all deeds to Malibu real estate are traceable to "the land of Matthew Keller in the Topanga Malibu Sequit."

Mr. Keller was born in Ireland and came to America at an early date. After living in Mexico for a time he came to California and settled in Los Angeles about 1850, becoming one of its best known and most prominent citizens. He was one of the first to engage in wine-making and to plant out an extensive vineyard, for which he imported stock from France.

"Extending from a place called 'Topanga,' the dividing line between these lands and the Ranch of 'Santa Monica,' on the southeast, along the Pacific to a point called Mugu on the northwest, and bounded on the northeast by a ledge of rocks on the top of and extending the whole length of a range of mountains; and adjoining the lines of the ranchos of 'Las Virgines,' 'Triunfo,' 'Santa Ysabel,' and 'Conejo."- decree, October 24, 1864

He devoted a great deal of attention to the cultivation of the grape and was also interested in the early experiments in raising cotton. At one time he had a complete ginning outfit set up in Downtown Los Angeles and offered its use to anyone who would raise cotton. He made a thorough study of the process of making wines of different varieties and manufactured it in large quantities and established trading houses in Los Angeles and San Francisco and was instrumental in introducing California wines in the east.

In 1862, when the cotton industry in the South was seriously disrupted by the Civil War, the CA State Legislature attempted to promote home production by offering a premium of $3,000 for the first 100 bales of cotton of 300 pounds each. For the 3 years following, premiums of $2,000, $1,000, and $500 were offered for the same amount. The Legislature, at its next meeting, qualified the original offer by stipulating that one-half or one-quarter of these premiums be paid for one-half or one- quarter of the amount originally named. No awards were made, apparently, until December 1865, when the State premium of $3,000 was given to *"Mr. Matthew Keller, Also known as Don Mateo Keller, of Los Angeles"*, who had grown his cotton on irrigated land.

MEDAL FOR GROWING COTTON; 1865. (T. CLEARY COLLECTION)

Many of his methods and scientific approaches to farming, are confirmed in his correspondence with Doctor Pierre Curie in France. At one point, he even planted oyster beds at the mouth of the Malibu River. But for the most part, Keller never developed Malibu, and leased it to cattle ranchers. He did plant many hundreds of acres of wine grapes near Solstice Canyon.

He put up a large ranch house on the Malibu Rancho and made improvements there and when he died in 1881 he left that grant to his son, Henry W. Keller, formerly of Santa Monica, who sold it in 1891 to the late Frederick H. Rindge.

Thirteen

A ticking time bomb tempts Playa Del Rey

Along and with the Ballona Wetlands, Hastings Canyon and Cabora Road represent the last areas of undeveloped land in Playa Del Rey. Much of the Cabora Road area was leased to local farmers by the government and Hughes Aircraft after WWII; who farmed there for generations. Also, much of the area is adjacent to, or set on one of the largest underground storage areas of natural gas in the country. It is owned by the Southern California Gas Company (Sempra Energy), who purchased it in 1953.

To help the war effort, it had been condemned by the Federal Government in 1942. Oil too has played a significant role here, or near here, as well. Exploration was begun in 1921 and abandoned in1925. The oil is contained in a sedimentary rock layer called: schist, and when deeper wells were drilled in 1929; the area began producing oil. The wells played out in the 1940's, and hundreds of wells were capped off. About 240 acres is now used for underground natural gas storage. But, methane gas leaks present a regular and potentially volatile nuisance, emitting record levels of highly flammable methane gas. High levels of methane are migrating into nearby neighborhoods, though all data collected thus far shows the combustible gas at depths just 40 feet underground, it often reaches ground level and is said to contain: benzene, toluene and xylene, also known carcinogens

OIL WELLS ON THE BEACH, 1920's. Bergman-Bright Oil Company (left) drilling headquarters, just off the lagoon. All over Playa Del Rey and Venice, oil wells dotted the sandy beaches. Oil production reached its peak in the 1920's. One can only imagine the obstacles they would encounter with the California Coastal Commission if they tried to drill oil on the beaches today. The photo on the right is at Toes Beach, south of Ballona Creek. (Courtesy, USC Libraries).

As I said, the wells were "capped off." The area below the bluffs and running out to the sea was once a huge prehistoric embayment, and as the water receded rich oil deposits were left there. There were HUNDREDS of wells along the shoreline, but many of these; about 300 wells, were drilled <u>on</u> the Del Rey Hills: just east of Falmouth and Manchester Boulevard. For a map of this field, see: **ftp://ftp.consrv.ca.gov/pub/oil/maps/Map_S-1.pdf**.

The oil wells were simply "plugged" with a few feet of gahnite (plaster), and homes were developed on the sites. It is unclear to me if disclosure of the well locations was in fact made to new home buyers who began snatching up the homes in the 1950's, 60's and 70's, however I am 99% sure that remediation of the soil surrounding the wells was never correctly achieved. And residents who moved here did so at a great risk, and in certain circles, whispers of early aggressive cancers and other health ailments are heard amongst grieving families. Many of my close friends have suffered losses. There are also strange tales of: paint peeling off walls, sick pets, flowers and shrubs dying, overpowering-putrid odors, concrete buckling, skin rashes and other allergy issues.

And it is not only the oil contamination that presents a problem. Groundwater may also be affected by the thousands of wells in Playa Del Rey- drilled for water, or for oil and gas exploration. When improperly drilled or cased, or when the casing has corroded, old oil, gas, and water wells serve as conduits for contamination of the aquifers below. Improperly completed and abandoned water wells may allow direct access from the surface to groundwater for contaminants such as pesticides, or they may facilitate the commingling of groundwater from one aquifer to another; a safety hazard to humans and pets. Abandoned oil wells are also channels for the upward movement of brine—salt water, often found in oil-bearing zones—and they are paths to contamination by oil and gas, drilling fluids, and other contaminants. For instance, salt water from abandoned oil wells has already polluted the upper portions of the Colorado River. These wells must be plugged to prevent the contamination of aquifers by salt water and oil wastes.

CABORA ROAD AND HASTINGS CANYON; PLAYA DEL REY. (Courtesy Google Images).

The chemicals used during the oil-well drilling process and disposed of in these pits include such highly toxic elements as barium, arsenic, and cadmium.

Every oil and gas well within the Playa Del Rey Oilfield, whether active or abandoned, urgently needs to be evaluated for well leakage problems. A properly implemented soil gas monitoring program, including the use of deep soil gas probes, is necessary for this purpose. In addition, a careful review needs to be made of the well records, including well histories regarding leakage, and evidence of seal failures. -- BEFORE THE PUBLIC UTILITIES COMMISSION OF THE STATE OF CALIFORNIA, Case 00-05-010 (Filed May 11, 2000).

But despite all of these potential health hazards, the remaining vacant land along the Playa Del Rey Bluffs/Westchester/Playa Vista, was developed with million to multimillion dollar homes. In 2001, Bernard Endres, PhD, an Oil and Gas Environmental Consultant, warned, "SoCalGas records indicate that billions of cubic feet of natural gas are being held at extremely high pressure in the partially depleted oil field that spans the (Playa Del Rey/Playa Vista) area. Of the approximately 300 sites in the United States where flammable gas is stored in the ground," Endres stated, "I could not find one over which a municipality was actively promoting the construction of housing. There is just too great a risk of catastrophic accident."

In 1992, in Brenham, Texas, an underground gas storage catastrophe did occur, killing several people. According to Endres, it was fortunate the Brenham explosion occurred in a rural area. "If it had been a densely populated development such as Playa Vista, hundreds if not thousands would have been killed and property damage would be incalculable," he warned. "For Los Angeles to approve housing so near the SoCalGas site is highly questionable and I urge City Council to reconsider further area development. This is no place for people to live."

Fourteen
One of the really good guys in early Los Angeles: Walter Trask

Only the veterans of the area remember when the street named for Walter Trask: Trask Avenue, in Playa Del Rey, opened on November 25, 1925, and that for many years that it intersected Century Boulevard. In those days, Century Boulevard ran all the way to the sea.

WALTER J. TRASK

An associate of R. C. Gillis, and an attorney, Minnesota native Trask was embroiled in a viscous fight between the Cities of Santa Monica with Collis Huntington, and San Pedro and the old Phineas Banning interests, regarding the relocation of the Port of Los Angeles; which was originally located at Port Ballona: now called Playa Del Rey.

In 1890, John D. Bicknell joined Trask and formed a law firm, and specialized in railroad law. In 1897 Judge James Gibson joined the firm and it eventually became Gibson, Dunn & Crutcher. Both firms represented the interests of Henry Huntington who controlled the railways in Los Angeles, including the Playa del Rey lines. He was a director the First National Bank of Los

Angeles, and the President of the Los Angeles Bar Association in 1910, and an avid member of Archaeological Institute of America, and was a life member of the Southwest Society; along with General Harrison Gray Otis, Chairman, and J. S. Slauson, President.

THE TRASK HOUSE, SANTA MONICA, CA; LATER CALLED THE KYTE HOUSE

Some locals might remember his 15,000 sq. ft. mansion in Santa Monica; it was The Chronicle Restaurant at 2624 Main Street. A gourmet restaurant in a restored Victorian house that was formerly located at the corner of Ocean Avenue and Washington Boulevard. Built in 1894 and once known as the Kyte House, in 1976 it was moved to its present location along with the adjoining Roy Jones House to form Heritage Square. Today it is called *the Victorian*, and can be rented for weddings and special events. For details, call: 310-392- 4956.

THE CHRONICLE RESTAURANT

Trask was known by everyone to be a true gentle man, and an avid fan of early California history. Suffering from poor health, Trask had moved from Minnesota for the better climate, but died suddenly in 1911.

Fifteen

Malibu; a cursed heritage

FREDERICK HASTINGS RINDGE.

Born in Cambridge, MA, in 1857, Frederick Rindge attended Harvard. He moved out to Los Angeles in 1887. Five years later, he became the final owner of the entire Rancho Malibu Spanish Land Grant, named *Rancho Topanga Malibu Simi Sequit* or "Malibu Rancho". At the time of his death, the *L.A. Times* reported the Rindge Ranch, devoted mainly to raising sheep, had grown to about 20,000 acres, stretching to a two and one-half miles wide at some points. The ranch house had burned down in 1903, and Rindge never got the chance to rebuild, and lived in a tent cabin when he was there.

The Curse of the Chumash haunts the place. The Indians were there first—as early as 3000 B.C. By A.D. 1000 the Chumash had taken over the region. They were energetic fishermen and traders who made elegant baskets and seven-man oceangoing plank canoes. The Spaniards arrived in 1542, and the Indians they neglected to slaughter were exterminated by birth control—Chumash males were forced by the mission fathers to live apart from their wives. In revenge, some say, Chumash medicine men laid a curse on all who would possess "Maliwu" after they were gone.

The first to take possession was Don José Bartolomé Tapia, who in 1802 was granted royal "permisión" to graze cattle on a 16,000-acre tract he called Rancho Topanga Malibu Simi Sostomo Sequit. But Tapia lost the authorizing document and had to fight off a long challenge to his rights. In 1848 Tapia's widow sold the ranch to her grandson-in-law, Leon Victor Prudhomme, for 400 pesos—200 in coin, 200 in "goods." Hard-pressed during the panic of 1857, Prudhomme sold out to an Irishman known as Don Mateo Keller—for $1,400. That's .10 cents an acre folks.

Keller escaped the curse. A graduate of Dublin's Trinity College who spoke five languages, he planted vineyards and was soon shipping 250,000 gallons of wine a year. He also cultivated grapes and crops in downtown Los Angeles. Eleven years after Keller's death in 1881, Rancho Malibu was sold for $172,000 to a Boston insurance magnate named Frederick Hastings Rindge, and the curse revived. Rindge was a Harvard graduate who envisioned "the Malibu" as an American Riviera that would someday rival in splendor the Côte d'Azur. But Malibu was very isolated; the Pacific Coast Highway had not yet been built.

But Rindge died in 1905, leaving his widow beset by bands of cattle rustlers and powerful interests that wanted to cut a highway up the coast; and to hell with the beauty of the place.

A tight-jawed, pistol-packin' mama, Rhoda May Rindge hired a small army of desperadoes to protect her empire, but in 1925 she lost her fight to block the highway and the next year, hard up for cash, she leased some beach lots for cottages. She and her husband built the Adamson House. The highway was built as the Roosevelt Highway, and later renamed Pacific Coast Highway. Modern Malibu was born.

The Adamson House grounds are open daily from 8:00 am to Sunset.

Now an enclave to the rich and famous, the area has suffered through storms and raging wild fires, but remains one of the best addresses on the planet.

Sixteen

The 1924 Hotel Del Rey Disaster, Playa Del Rey, California

On June 2, 1924, about 11PM, a Pacific Electric "Red" Streetcar made its last stop for the evening, at the present day intersection of Vista Del Mar and Culver Boulevards in Playa Del Rey. One passenger exited the trolley, carrying two five- gallon tin cans or coal oil, and made her way silently across the sandy lagoon shoreline approaching the former site of the Del Rey Hotel—now a school for girls. The area was unlit, and on this moonless night she was nearly invisible to locals.

The lagoon site was once the location of large tourist attraction; hosting boat races, fishing derbies, and even bowling. But the Pavilion burned before the war, and the Del Rey Hotel, which had become a house of prostitution, had been shuttered in 1917, as angry Los Angeleno's had forced its closure.

But the building reopened as *The Hope Development School for Retarded Children* (for girls), in about 1920. Mrs. J.C. Thomas was the matron of the home. The area was off the beaten path, and the doors and windows were routinely locked at night. Also, the children's bedrooms were locked to keep them from roaming the hallways.

The recalcitrant 14-year-old old Josephine Bertholme, mentally challenged and recently expelled from the school for continued violent acts; and who was living alone in a Sawtelle area day-room, struggled with the cans of volatile coal oil as she approached the hotel.

The Hotel Del Rey was located at the north end of the Del Rey Lagoon.

Bertholme first checked that the front door was indeed locked, and doused the dry and decaying wooden porch with one can of oil, and then headed to the back porch; and emptied the contents of the second can. After igniting the fire, she moved across the street to sit on a sand dune, at what is now Toes Beach--and watched the blaze. In the end, 22 girls would perish in the fire, along with Mrs. Thomas and her young adopted son, who was asleep in a crib at the foot of her bed.

School Mistress Lola May Rademaker did manage to rescue 19 screaming children, who sat in the sand in charred night-clothes; many of them badly burned, and who also watched in complete horror as the structure burned to the ground. Many of the survivors would later report seeing Bertholme, "Laughing at the destruction from across the road." Leaving the fire by walking down to Venice Beach, Bertholme would confess to the killings two weeks later. Some of the girls jumped into the Lagoon, a virtual cesspool, to sooth their blackened and blistered bodies; later dying from staph infection-- and not from the burns.

The charred bodies of the victims were stacked like kindling wood on the dunes, and waited; swelling in the heat, for a truck or wagon to be sent from the coroner's office in Downtown Los Angeles.

Today. the location is marked by a small park, just outside the left field fence at Del Rey/ American Little League's: Krauch Field, Del Rey Lagoon, Playa Del Rey, CA.

Seventeen

Westchester/Playa Del Rey Landmarks

Not too long ago, I was driving through Central Pennsylvania on a meandering country road at a town called Peach Glen, PA. It is located a few miles from the revered Civil War battle field, and another town: Gettysburg. Just like at so many small towns, rising from the middle of a field was a tremendous water tower with the name of the town painted proudly on the side. Many of our SOCAL neighbors still relish their water towers too.

I started making a list of what we might consider the most significant landmark in our town. The often forgotten **Centinela Adobe**: one of the birthplaces of modern **Rancho's La Ballona/Centinela** came to mind. Certainly **LAX**, if you could call it a landmark would have to head the list. And of course that would include the historic **Mines Field Terminal**, the **Theme Building**: home of the **Encounter Restaurant**, and the dazzling **LAX Gateway Pylon Project**. Did you know the original runways at LAX; our 1928 Mine's Field, were made of adobe?

THE LAX GATEWAY PYLON PROJECT, by artist Paul Tzanetopoulos, was installed in 2000. This work is a kinetic light installation that is incorporated into twenty-six large-scale translucent glass towers. Eleven towers are 6' in diameter, ranging from 25 to 60 feet down Century Boulevard and fifteen towers are 12' diameter by 100' located at the Los Angeles International Airport gateway traffic intersection exchange. All towers are synchronized and computer-driven with lighting interface. The programming consists of lighting display, synchronous lighting activities and color arrays.

PHOTO, Right: The LAX Theme Building designed by Pereira & Luckman architect <u>Paul Williams</u> and constructed in 1961, resembles a flying saucer that has landed on its four legs.

A few miles up the road, at **Loyola Marymount University**, a large *L* was left on the bluff below by a construction company when the Loyola campus was completed in 1929, and was converted into an *LMU* in 1973 in recognition of the merger with Marymount College. And for that matter, the **Playa Del Rey/Westchester Bluffs**; remnants of an ancient marine terrace on upper Pleistocene sand dunes might qualify as a landmark all by themselves.

By definition, a landmark is an object, (as a stone or tree), that marks the boundary of land or a conspicuous object on land that marks a locality. There are many signs and markers welcoming folks to the area. Some are located near our **Downtown Westchester Shopping District**, the **Westchester Recreation Center**; which sits near our last bowling alley, **Eldorado Bowl**. Uptown Westchester alone is the home of the old **Loyola** and **Paradise** movie houses and the former **Broadway/Miliron's Department Store.** Enclosed beneath the concrete and covered by brass markers; almost like eerie tombstones, the Paradise Theater building sidewalk holds relics from the bygone days of motion pictures, patiently waiting for folks to come and visit again.

The Paradise Theatre in Westchester was located a few blocks south of the Fox Loyola Theater. It opened in 1950. The front is of field-stone, brick and glass in the modern California style. Live plants under the canopy gave this area an outdoor patio effect. After passing through a mirrored and planted lobby with a curved refreshment stand and a manager's office at one side, the patron entered a magnificent foyer with pastel walls trimmed in redwood and aquamarine carpeting studded with yellow and beige stars. The last chain to operate the Paradise Theater was Pacific Theaters, and it later ran as an independent for a short time before being gutted and turned into an office building. Along with a few high school pals, such as former Playa Del Rey resident, and co-promoter of the Annual Gillis Beach Volleyball Tourney: Dave Cressman, I worked as an usher at the Paradise. We spent the summer of 1972 sneaking friends into movies. PHOTO, Right: Mines Field, 1933. The name came from real estate agent William W. Mines who represented the ranching interests and he claimed his own bit of history when he clinched the deal. For years Angelinos refused to call their airport anything else. The city leased 640 acres for ten years and aviation got an immediate boost when America's 1928 National Air Races brought the crowds flocking to Mines Field to see pilots like the legendary Charles Lindbergh. Communications consisted of two "trunk" telephone lines, two-way radio and on-field weather reports. Modern hotels and restaurants were in the city, but a restaurant was on the field. Buses ran hourly, and the taxi rate for the 11 miles to the city was 50 cents.

Playa Del Rey town signs are few, and like Plays Del Rey, they hide and blend in with the rest of the west-side of Los Angeles. **Dockweiler State Beach** surrounds the town to the west, and the historical **Del Rey Lagoon**, marks the boundary between the **Marina Del Rey** and **Ballona Creek**; the former **Los Angeles River** on the north. And of course the **Playa Del Rey Wetlands** celebrates the easterly boundary of the town, not far from the near-coastal bluffs and what was once called **Mount Ballona.**

Playa del Rey Lagoon, 1902, with Mount Ballona rising above the coastline. The capital *D* in *De*l Rey was added many years later. At the base of the hill today sits Tanners Coffee Company. (PHOTO: complements, Wikipedia).

Henry David Thoreau wrote: "We should come home from adventures, and perils, and discoveries every day with new experience and character." We all define "home" differently and it means many things to many people. I think home, and your home-town is a place that you enjoy, love and toil hard and fight for; and worship at and raise children from. You try to give a little back to your town along the way, and make a friend or two, and visit the local merchants and eateries and enjoy the landmarks and special places it has to offer.

The roads of Playa Del Rey and Westchester are familiar to me and it is almost always enjoyable to be back. If I missed a landmark that is a special place for you in town, drop me a line.

Eighteen
The Los Angeles Hyperion

Opened in the late 1800's, and located on the bluffs above the beach at Imperial Highway and Vista Del Mar, the city installed a "screening system" in 1925. Prior to that time, and since 1894, raw/untreated sewage was dumped directly into the Santa Monica Bay(at Playa Del Rey), through an offshore pipe, called an outfall, outraging local swimmers.

THE LOS ANGELES HYPERION WORKS, PLAYA DEL REY, 1925.

In 1888, a prominent figure, Juan Carillo canvassed the La Ballona residents, now Playa Del Rey and Playa Vista, and succeeded in stopping the construction of a second outfall at Pier Avenue and Venice Boulevard.

WOMEN OF THE LOS ANGELES COUNTY AUXIALLRY POLICE PATROL, GILLIS BEACH, PLAYA DEL REY, 1942.

During WWII, the outfall pipe cracked. THE L.C.A.P. was employed to enforce curfews, quarantines and spot for enemy aircraft. Local beaches were restricted, and were used as military encampments to prepare for possible Japanese invasion. One such gun emplacement was set on the dunes, across the street from the Hyperion. Due to a vast sewage spill, the beaches were closed for many years, beginning in 1942.

NEW PIPE, PLAYA DEL REY HYPERION, 1947. Sections of 12-foot pipe being used in new outfall sewer line, to help eliminate pollution of beaches. The new outfall line and an intensive chlorination program may reopen quarantined beaches. Up to 21 tons of chlorine will be used daily to treat the sewage output. Playa Del Rey was still experiencing complete closures as late as February, 1947.

Today, the Los Angeles Hyperion has installed many new technologically driven systems to prevent raw sewage entering into Santa Monica Bay at Dockweiler State Beach.

The water is as pure as drinking water when it enters the ocean.

Nineteen

Escaping to the madness:

daily commutes to and from the beach cities

PLAYA DEL REY MAP-THOMAS BROTHERS PAGE 31, 1956

I am sorry if this map is hard to read. I think the most important issue is the elimination of two vital east/west routes that used to help funnel traffic away from Playa Del Rey and other beach communities.

Imperial Highway of course is a key road; and now joins the Century Freeway: Route 105 at Sepulveda Boulevard. However, Manchester and Culver Boulevards remain the only ways to make your east/west daily trek from paradise to the interior of Los Angeles.

Two key commuter roads were lost(along with well over half the neighborhood), when LAX expanded; **Century Boulevard and Ocean Vista Street**, the latter which joined with Inglewood Parkway.

Beginning now at Pershing Boulevard, the improved Manchester Parkway has helped to ease the congestion and bottlenecks that occur at Playa Del Rey on Culver Boulevard, but this "band-aid" of a street will eventually just dump you onto Sepulveda Boulevard at Uptown Westchester, which after all is no solution at all.

And of course the fact that Speedway Boulevard; that used to cross the Ballona Creek, (and was a well traveled north/south route to Venice and Santa Monica), was closed when the Marina was built, didn't help things.

Twenty

El Porto: quirky but well loved;
a former County Island

Beginning in the early 1900's, the beach towns of Los Angeles were developed with fervor. A man named George H. Peck subdivided El Porto. CA, in 1911. There were 83 business lots and 225 residential lots; on good soil partly covered with large trees and ocean view sand lots. Included were concrete sidewalks, curbs and oiled streets. An artesian well was drilled, and piped in to the homes.

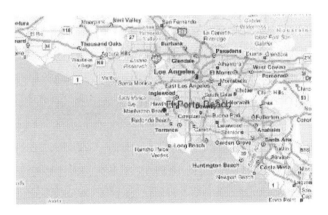

MAP OF EL PORTO, CA

According to Wikepedia, although it is thought to mean "The Port" in Spanish, the name is actually a misspelling and translates "The I Carry." The Spanish word for port should have actually been spelled p-u-e-r-t-o. However, "porto" is the Portuguese word for "port," but its article is "O" instead of "El," which leads one to believe the origin of the name El Porto could have come from both Spanish and Portuguese influences.

The boundary of El Porto is 45th Street on the north side, which is the border with El Segundo, and its Chevron oil refinery, to 38th Street, which was the old border with Manhattan; the east-west boundary is Crest Drive, next to the fence of El Segundo's oil refinery, to El Porto State Beach and the Pacific Ocean.

The commercial section of El Porto is along Highland Avenue, which is its only main thoroughfare. North of 45th Street, Highland becomes Vista Del Mar Boulevard, which runs along the coast to Playa Del Rey.

In November 1980, the unincorporated town of El Porto, consisting of approximately 34 acres (140,000 m^2) and a population of about 1,185 people, was annexed from the County of Los Angeles by Manhattan Beach. For over 60 years, El Porto was a county island, and the residents attended the El Segundo school system.

A county island is an unincorporated area within a county , usually, but not always, surrounded on all sides by another city. On maps, these geopolitical anomalies will form jagged or complex borders and 'holes' in the city limits. Generally found more frequently out west, county islands form in areas of expansion when previously smaller cities will annex and incorporate more land into their jurisdiction. If residents or landowners in a particular unincorporated area do not vote to incorporate with the surrounding city, the area remains unincorporated. The formation of a county island usually follows stages where it will come into being on the edge of an incorporated area, and as more territory is incorporated, be cut off from the rest of the unincorporated area within the county. These areas are not, by definition, exclaves because they are simply unincorporated within a surrounding city.

Local surfer Randy Wright taming a bitchen wave at El Porto

As far as surfing goes, Jay Kazner of Surfline says:

"With more personalities than Sibyl, El Porto has maintained its reputation more due to easy parking than any outstanding wave quality. El Porto's a northwest swell magnet, however, and is almost always bigger than any other spot in the South Bay during the winter months. The trick is to find the zone with the "holes," as the locals call it, referring to breaks in the relentless closeouts up and down the beach. With spring sandbars or a crossed swell, the place can get real good, except that everyone's on it before you can feed your meter. In past years, the area has taken hits from "beach nourishment" programs, wherein tons of sand were trucked in, turning the area into the Great Wall of China. There is also terrible water quality, some say because of years of hydrocarbons leaching through the sand from the nearby Chevron refinery. The place does, at times, get machine-like, at least where the smell is concerned."

Hey we like it here!

Stay local and get your El Porto gear at:

Twenty-one

Actress Mae Murray;

Down and Out in Playa Del Rey

Mae Murray, 1889-1965:
"The Girl With The Bee-Stung Lips."

Murray became a star of the club circuit in both the United States and Europe, performing with Clifton Webb, Rudolph Valentino, and John Gilbert as some of her many dance partners. She made many films; and her most-famous role was probably in the Erich von Strohem directed film The Merry Widow (1925), opposite John Gilbert. However, when silent movies gave way to talkies, Murray's voice proved not to be compatible with the new sound, and her career began to fade.

At her career peak in the early 1920s, Murray, along with such other notable Hollywood personalities as Cecil B. DeMille (who later became her neighbor in Playa Del Rey), Douglas Fairbanks Sr. and Irving Thalberg, was a member of the board of trustees at the Motion Picture & Television Fund, a charitable organization that offers assistance and care to those in the motion picture and television industries without financial resources. She made many career mistakes however, but somehow managed to squeak out a living for many years.

Murray built an enormous mansion on the sand at 64th Avenue and Ocean Front Walk; across the street from the Del Rey Lagoon, and a few yards from Ballona Creek; quite literally at the estuary of the creek and the location of the former Port Ballona. Her beachfront parties were attended by a virtual Who's Who in Hollywood; lasting days at a time. Apparently she owned stock in some of the oil wells that were located in her own back yard.

A view of the Mae Murray mansion at Playa Del Rey, CA.

By 1933 however, she was broke herself, and ordered by the court to sell her opulent Playa del Rey estate to pay a judgment against her, and her life was never the same. Moving to New York to find work, she was arrested for vagrancy; found sleeping on a park bench. When she returned to California, she was often seen wandering the streets of Playa Del Rey and sitting on the beach near her former home.

In 1964, living off charity and devoted friends, the poor deluded Murray continually traveled by transcontinental bus from coast to coast on a self promoted publicity tour, hoping for a comeback in movies.

On the last of these excursions, she lost herself during a stopover in Kansas City, Missouri, and wandered to St. Louis. The Salvation Army found her on the streets, and sent her back to Los

Angeles. She rented a small Hollywood apartment near the Chinese Theatre, paid for by actor George Hamilton.

It has been speculated that the character Norma Desmond in Sunset Boulevard (1950), a washed-up silent superstar living in self-delusion, and who bragged about her wealth and ownership in producing oil wells was based on Mae Murray, but the writers of the film: Billy Wilder and Charles Bracket would never admit it. The William Holden character, opposite Gloria Swanson, was named Joe Gillis.

Mae Murray passed away in 1965, at The Motion Picture House in Woodland Hills, California, the place that she helped to found.

Twenty-Two

Benjamin "Don Benito" Wilson

RANCHO LA BALLONA RE-DIVIDED, MAY 1868.

BENJAMIN DAVIS WILSON, 1870. (Courtesy, Google Books).

The re-division of the Rancho was driven partly by several lawsuits that had been filed against the Talamantes Family, including a lawsuit filed, after California became a State, by the second elected Mayor of Los Angeles, Benjamin "Don Benito" Wilson*.

Wilson had loaned one of the owners of the land $1,500.00 at an interest rate of 60% per annum, and when they defaulted, he received one-quarter of the Rancho. However the award. (¼ of 14,000 acres) was deemed insufficient to cover the loan!

 Impatient to collect, he sold his note to Messrs. George Sanford and John Young for $5,000.00, and they went to court to claim their land. The Rancho, along with most of Los Angeles, had been ravaged by drought(9 of 10 cattle died), floods and epidemic diseases.

In 1868, a judge decided which portions of Rancho La Ballona were the most valuable; and the closer you were to Ballona Creek, the more valuable the land.

The judge decided the fairest way to divide the land was to give each owner: (1) a portion of the most valuable land, and (2) the least valuable farmland. The judge decided the most valuable land was along Ballona Creek; it had water. Next was farmland that could be irrigated, and then pasture.

The present day streets of Lincoln and Culver Boulevard's represent several of the boundaries in the 1868 settlement, and eventually road construction and city limits followed those established lines.

It is one of the reasons those two streets are so crooked.

*Wilson discovered and named Big Bear Lake. He was the Grandfather of WWII General George S. Patton, and Mount Wilson is named for him.

Twenty-Three
The Motordome at
Playa Del Rey, California-1910

The Los Angeles Coliseum Motordome at Playa Del Rey

(Note the un-channelized Ballona Creek in the background)

In 1910, an ex-bicycle racer and promoter, named Jack Prince sold an investor on the idea of building a wooden speedway at Playa del Rey. It was built next to Speedway Boulevard, which was one of the first developed roads in Los Angeles. Speedway is the current day Culver Boulevard.

The famous race-car driver *Barney Oldfield immediately did a lap at the amazing speed of 99 miles an hour.

The track was made from thousands of boards, held together by tons of nails. Prince's first design was a one-mile circular bowl with steep sloped sides. The track was extremely dangerous, and the public cheered as fatalities mounted.

On April 7, 1911, Don Johns, riding a standard-valve Indian Motorcycle, burst into the national headlines when he shattered all amateur records from 2 to 20-miles. In the process, he tied Ray Seymour's professional record for the mile and broke the world record for the 2-mile distance. Riding for Team Excelsior, the nationally-acclaimed rider set an official world record for the mile on the Playa del Rey board track. Despite a wind that "would snatch the fillings from your teeth," Johns turned a 39 and 2/5th-second time for the distance, replacing his former mentor, Jake Drossier, as the title holder. Johns was 16-years old. He was four-feet ten inches tall, and weighed around ninety pounds.

Don Johns

Finally, in 1913, a fire destroyed the track; and Damon Runyan wrote, "Playa del Rey burned last night with a great saving of lives."

Barney Oldfield* (#1), Turn 3, at the Motordome

*(Oldfield died in 1946, and is buried a few blocks away at nearby Holy Cross Cemetery, in Culver City, CA).

LOS ANGELES TRACK WILL OPEN FRIDAY; New Motordrome Will Hold Seven-Day Racing Carnival with All the Crack Drivers.

April 3, 1910, Sunday
Section: SPORTING SECTION

Friday will see the opening of the Los Angeles Motordrome at Playa del Rey, six miles from Los Angeles, Cal. The inauguration of the board track with a seven days' carnival marks a new epoch in automobile racing and judging from the phenomenal speed made in practice by drivers, all the world's records for mile tracks and many motordrome marks as well, are likely to be broken.

Twenty-Four

Cruising the Westside,
and stopping for a Patmar burger

PATMARS DRIVE-IN, MOTEL AND RESTAURANT-1940's

Driving along Sepulveda Boulevard near LAX today, it's hard to believe that there was ever so much vacant land; but this photo of Patmars Drive-In, at Sepulveda Boulevard and Imperial Highway, shows us just how much LAX has grown up since then.

For many years Patmars was a favorite stop for locals and tourists alike, but was probably most frequented by the Douglas Aircraft company employees.

With plants all over Southern California, including Santa Monica and LAX, World War II was a major earner for Douglas. The company produced almost 30,000 aircraft from 1942 to 1945 and the workforce swelled to 160,000. The company produced a number of aircraft including the C-47 (based on the DC-3), the DB-7 (known as the A-20, Havoc or Boston), the Dauntless and the A-26 Invader.

Local folks speak about Patmars in an American-Graffiti sort-of homage; a place where local high school kids took their dates for a soda and a burger, before and after a little cruising on Hawthorne Boulevard.

Just up Sepulveda at Manchester Boulevard in Westchester, was another favorite spot with the poodle-skirters: Tiny Naylors, where car-hops roller-skated to your car window.

Tiny Naylor's was just across the street from the Loyola theatre. Before this former Westchester theater's conversion to a medical office building, the front of the Loyola featured a beautiful swan that rose about sixty feet above the theater's marquee. The auditorium was similar to the Fox Crest Theater in North Long Beach, CA.

Twenty-Five
Westchester California's Own Surf Band

While the Beach Boys were honing their craft, a few miles up the road in Hawthorne, CA, another group was getting ready to burst onto the music scene in Westchester.

Former site of Westchester Music; the Banner Carpet store was torn down to make way for The Parking Spot, at Sepulveda Boulevard and Manchester Parkway.

For years local residents relied on Westchester Music Store, located at Sepulveda Boulevard and Wil Rogers Street, to supply them with records and musical instruments. I actually still have several vinyl albums from the old music store, including **The Beatles** *Rubber Soul*, and **Love**, *Forever Changes,* to mention a few. I do not know what happened to the hundreds of '45's my brothers and sister bought there. Many local kids took music lessons there from a man called Mr. Ferguson, who gave clarinet lessons in a drafty cubicle above the Westchester Music Store. Two local kids, Mark Volman who went to Orville Wright Jr. High and Howard Kaylan who went to Airport Jr. High (now Hertz Rent-A-Car on Airport Boulevard), were taking music lessons there on the clarinet and saxophone.

Later at Westchester High School, A Capella Choir, which was conducted by Mr. Robert Wood, was formed. Mark was a first tenor, Howard a second tenor. (Wood was so influential that the duo later named a publishing company after him; *Mr. Woods Music*. It was quite a choir, and won all sorts of city competitions.

In 1963, Al Nichol, Howard Kaylan, and Chuck Portz had just changed the name of their novice surf combo from the **Nightriders** to the **Crossfires**. Mark Volman knew them from the Westchester High choir and joined the group (initially as a roadie). Also in the band were Don Murray from Inglewood High and Dale Walton. Dale was later replaced by Tom Stanton, who in turn, was later replaced by Jim Tucker. Ironically, their music was almost exclusively instrumental! Four guys from choir forming an instrumental band? Actually, it wasn't all that surprising. In 1962, the hardest dance music of the time evolved out of **Dick Dale's** concept of the *Surfer Stomp*, searing guitar solos over a pounding rhythm section. Nichol was one of the very best of the city's surf guitarist, and The Crossfires adapted their own, original versions of standards like "Money" and "What'd I Say."

Here they were, 15 year old kids, their fingers ripping away at their saxes, playing at fraternity parties, and being exposed to strangely devastating drinks like "Red Death," and all manner of mayhem. To rise to the occasion, and to keep the frat boys happy and paying them $200-a-night jobs (good money for 1962), the Crossfires adapted their own, original versions of standards like "Money" and "What'd I Say" that were laced with the well chosen obscenities that the UCLA party boys loved so much. An ill-timed rendition of those very same ditties at the Westchester Women's Club effectively banned the Crossfires from Westchester, for good.

The Crossfires performing at the

King's Jewelry 37th Anniversary Grand Re-opening, 1963.

Except to true surf-music aficionados, The Crossfires, like so many surf bands of the period have fallen into obscurity. But this was no regular group of musicians. In 1964, the Beatles and the whole English Invasion took the United States by storm, and Mark and Howard put down their saxes, took up the vocals and the Crossfires dropped their entire repertoire of surf instrumentals and grew their hair long.

And the group became one of the greatest American bands of all times, with hits like *Happy Together* and *You Know She'd Rather Be With Me.*

You know them as, **The Turtles**.

Twenty-Six

Often imitated but never equaled; the Shack at Playa Del Rey

Located next to the former California Bar and Grill: the home of the first bank in Playa Del Rey (about 1904), sits Culver Boulevard's and Playa Del Rey's mainstay burger-bar: the Shack. To understand Playa Del Rey and the local scene, you must first drop into the shack for one of their famous and undeniably delicious burgers and side of onion rings or golden brown French fries.

It is of course a triple bypass with a side of coronary, but when the food craze beckons you, head on done to The Shack. Follow it up with an iced cold draft beer from their generous selections.

If you want to know the people of this great beach town, this is the place to start.

Twenty-Seven

Stones

I was asked at a neighborhood block party, why I had not written my column last month for the Westchester Hometown News. My friend liked the piece regarding The Spruce Goose, but, I dunno', maybe he was the only one that read it.

As it was last spring and summer, those months were very busy for me, so there was little time for writing. I traveled over 16000 miles, primarily back and forth from the Mid-West- Chicago, South Bend, and Cincinnati, and through much of Michigan. Finally: Seattle, Portland and Vancouver, British Columbia. Being on the road this much, home only 4 days in 29, can be quite an exigent professional task, (In fact, I am writing this at an airport gate at Seattle-Tacoma airport.)

When you return home and you finally get back to your own roads and see the road signs announcing your return to Westchester it is a nice feeling. It's as familiar and good as holding hands with the one you love or a baby's smile, the morning fog off Playa Del Rey, your kid hitting a Little League baseball homer, and the sounds of your children's laughter or a full stocking on Christmas morning.

There are several road signs welcoming folks to Westchester: at Lincoln and Sepulveda Boulevards, and up and down Manchester. One sign sits near the Westchester Vietnam Memorial at the corner of Lincoln and Manchester. I learned upon my return that this site has to be moved, as vandals, allegedly high school students, have defaced it. I still am in disbelief that any person could desecrate a War Memorial. They might as well have spit on the American Flag. These are the same type of people that: like to kick dogs, will grow up and beat their children-and teach them to disrespect consecrated public property. You cannot justify this as just the actions of immature thoughtless youth.

The Memorial stands for the many Westchester and Playa Del Rey residents that fought and died in battle: Tet, Operation Deckhouse Five, and Khe Sahn. There are real names: Richard, Victor, Dennis and Robert, and many others, carved into a stone memorial, all dead, and all once airport area residents. They died on maneuvers and on trails and in jungles and in places with no-names with a pack on their back and a rifle in their hand.

Westchester Vietnam Veterans Memorial.

I'd like to call some of my Vietnam Veteran buddies, and invite them to hang around the memorial some afternoon, and see just what kind of inhuman being could do this sort of thing. Maybe that is just what these punk's need - a visit from an Army Ranger, a Navy S.E.A.L., or Green Beret?

When I leave town on family vacations, we like to end up at a river or lake, and although I enjoy these trips, it is almost always nice to get home too. On these caravans, the morning is best when the rivers and lakes are calm-sitting there with a cup of hot coffee and warming by a new campfire- listening to a still-quiet morning, sometimes watching a river flow over rocks on its timeless-sacred-flowing journey-thinking of my own journey.

On the shorelines of these rivers and lakes, my children, from their very earliest ages, got in the habit of collecting small rocks and stones. At first, they would bring home three or four stones, but as time has gone along, they have become more selective-usually just bringing home one special stone each. My youngest son would stuff so many rocks in the pockets of his river-shorts that he could barely float in the water, but now he searches on and off all day for just a perfect one. In the process, he has again achieved buoyancy.

The stones are quartz and granite-smooth river rocks-some which winter frosts had heaved and broken in two-cut sharply as with the blade of a knife or saw. Many are veined or dotted with microcline and feldspar. Some are smooth- round and others rough and jagged. One is shaped like a small morel-colored russet and blue and copper. Another is jet black and the shape of a saddlebow. I have saved them all-as all of them represent a memory as long lasting as the rocks themselves.

This past May, while preparing for the aforementioned June travels, I collected all of the stones. I had stashed them in different places around the house and couldn't bear to part with them, although I never had any plans for them either.

In the wilderness, Indians and Frontiersmen would mark a trail by stacking stones with a stone pointing down trail-showing the way for other explorers and pioneers and sometimes military troops-leading them to forts and garrisons. These trail signs had various meanings-for instance, three stones stacked atop each other, means:" Danger, I need help!" Sometimes they would mark a trail by chopping cuts and slices into the bark of trees with an axe or knife: "Trail Blazes," mindful to cut only the bark-not harming the tree by piercing the wood flesh. Thus the term: "Trailblazing." These were the first road sings in America, and most followed well-known game and animal migration trails.

After doing my spring planting-tomato and flowers, I collected the stones and made trail signs with them in my garden. My own personal wilderness trail. I have placed blue stones atop red sandstone, and grey-flecked granite below brown and yellow river pebbles and white quartz. They are surrounded by flowers and flowering bushes and vines. It makes a fine display.

Now when I walk the brick-lined path through my backyard, restacking the stones that the winds have shifted, I happily play back these memories in my mind as if looking at a Kinescope or nickelodeon picture. I am reminded of Lake Naciemiento near Paso Robles and The Colorado River near Needles, and the gold-field streams near Sonora and the mighty Lake Mead. Three are from the barren Southwestern deserts of Nevada and Arizona. Another was plucked from a stream near Rainbow Falls, in Mammoth, while on a 12 mile hike. One is from Orlando, Florida.

Others are from the beaches of Playa Del Rey and Dockweiller Beach, and a few from a meandering stream in the Eastern Sierras near Bishop, and from the coastal foothills above Napa. There are several more from the shore of Bass Lake, just south of Wawona in Yosemite. A large one came from the dirt parking lot aside The Mission Santa Barbara, which we had used to chock our camper tires while we went to Mass there. We have also found a few ancient pottery shards in a stream near Independence.

Rocks and stones were belched from the bellies of the earth, the deep of the ocean and were castoff by the grinding and carving of great glaciers- made hard with the passing of time- washed by rain and pressure strengthened by layer upon layer of rich sediment-silt-sludge. Some have traveled the universe and to our solar system-crashing in a ball-of-fire, but finally cooling and becoming a part of our world. They have been chipped from the sides of the highest pristine mountains, and sandblasted by siroccos, and become tiny testaments, remaining to remind us of the greatness and the beauty of the Earth.

They remain proud-strong signs, all on their own.

My trail markers are welcome signs now, but moreover remind me of where we have been- hiked, boated, surfed, swam and made camp, and keep me wondering about when and where we will go next, and like the stones, the new strong memories yet to be made and found.

Finally, though, it is always good to be home again.

Twenty-eight

Daniel Freeman and the birth of Westchester,
(You can try all you want to, <u>Inglewood</u>, but the Adobe is in *WESTCHESTER*, 90045).

DANIEL FREEMAN, 1837-1918.

In 1863, a Scottish immigrant, Sir Robert Burnett, purchased Rancho Sausal Redondo and Rancho Aguaje De Centinela from the original land grant -heirs for $33,000. These included parts of Rancho La Ballona. Ten years later in 1873, Burnett leased the ranch to a Canadian, Daniel Freeman, and returned to Scotland. Freeman moved his wife and three children onto the ranch and started growing various crops.

On May 4, 1885 Freeman bought the ranch from Burnett for $140,000. Like Burnett before him, Freeman utilized the land for sheep ranching. It was a profitable business for a few years, but the drought of 1875-1876 brought on disastrous results.

About 22,000 head of Freeman's sheep died in that period. He decided to try dry-farming and helped to develop the Port Ballona area, shipping millions of bushels of barley from his wharf there. Remnants of the rail line built thru to the proposed (but never fully developed) Port Ballona went up to Santa Monica's Long Wharf. He would ultimately subdivide the rancho; having to sell off most of the land.

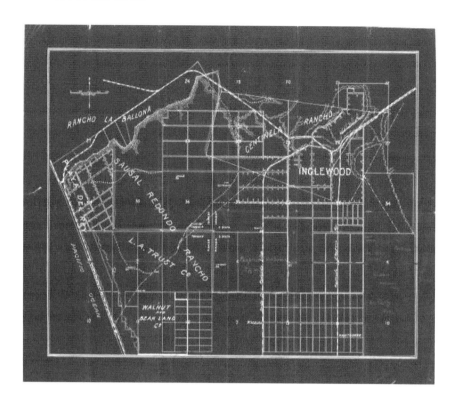

Twenty-nine

Ya' better get ready to tie up the boat in Idaho

LATEST MODEL OF WHAT PLAYA DEL REY AND PLAYA VISTA WILL LOOK LIKE AT THE END OF THE CENTURY.

'

Playa Del Rey/Playa Vista, California circa, 5000 B.P.

A report sponsored by the Governor of California Arnold Schwarzenegger and released today, finally warns about the impending disaster that will face numerous communities up and down the Pacific Coast. With sea levels rising as a result of global warming, the low lying areas at Playa Del Rey and Playa Vista, and all over the South Bay, may again return to inland bays.

And yet, people continue to attempt to build. Perhaps those same builders would be better served to begin construction of an ark; because we are going to need it.

In my book, Beach of the King, and at my Los Angeles Public Library exhibit, and in my local columns, I have consistently tried to point out the lunacy that that is being practiced in certain areas.

Specifically, parts of Playa Del Rey and all of Playa Vista were built on the site of an ancient embayment running over seven miles inland to the Baldwin Hills Bluffs. Native Americans, and early *Californios* regularly fought a battle with the sea and flooding rivers and creeks. It is after all, and remains, an alluvial plain. Just because you put a little lipstick on a pig, doesn't mean it isn't still a pig.

What we have done is to ignore what the area pioneers knew; namely that the great wetlands that once existed along our coasts should be respected for what they are, and that we should not try to make them into something that they are not.

Remember the Tongva parable of **The Coyote and the Water.**

This is *Before the Deluge.*

Thirty

Dining at Playa Del Rey

As far as I know, the first dining room was opened on the Del Rey Lagoon at the old **Pavilion at Playa Del Rey,** on Thanksgiving Day, 1904. It burned down before the First World War. Beginning in 1871, **William Tells' Lookout**, and later **Michael Duffy's Hunters Cottage** operated services for hunters that frequented the lagoon, but the services were Spartan; by and large, taverns. In 1905, the **Hotel Playa** which had opened on Speedway Boulevard, (today called Culver Boulevard), at more or less the location of Tanners Coffee Co., opened its Seaside Grill.

Ten years later, Christmas Eve Dinner 1916 at the **Hotel Playa** was quite an event. Of course compared to the numerous fine restaurants in the area today, a choice of <u>one</u> made planning quite simple. For the second time in 20 years, Playa Del Rey had fallen into ruins, and it was the only place open. But clinging to tradition, film stars and folks from Playa del Rey and all over Los Angeles came for the annual tree trimming gala and a seven course meal. Although the resort at Playa Del Rey had fallen into disrepair, trolley service still ran to the region, and the hotel, the only active remnant of the seaside extravaganza, was trying to persevere and stay in business. Notables such as Thomas Ince, D. W. Griffith and Mack Sennet frequented the hotel.

But, America would enter the war a few months later, and the area was nearly abandoned. Christmas 1916 was called by many, the "Last Innocent Christmas." By the War's end, over 115,000 Americans would lose their lives, and the landscape of the world changed forever.

CHRISTMAS EVE DINNER INVITATION, 1916. The Hotel Playa hosted an annual Christmas feast. In 1916, World War I was raging in Europe. The trolley fare from Santa Monica was five-cents. The Royal Air Force introduced the Sopwith Pup into action and a partial solar eclipse occurred on this day. The silent version of Jules Verne's' *20,000 Leagues Under the Sea*, starring Matt Moore, premiered in theatres, and *Oh How She Could Yacki, Hacki, Wicki Wacki, Woo*, was at the top of the music charts. Earlier in the year, Woodrow Wilson was reelected, and Kirk Douglas, Gregory Peck, Glenn Ford, Jackie Gleason, Dinah Shore, Dick Haymes and Betty Grable were born.

With the War and the destruction of the Amusements at Playa Del Rey, the Hotel Playa fell into disrepair and closed. A Minnesota native, and he himself having just returned with a Lieutenants rank from WWI, Fritz Burns, opened the Dickinson and Gillespie real estate headquarters there, and began to develop the new seaside communities of Del Rey Hills, Surfridge and Palisades del Rey.

MOUNT BALLONA, 1920's. The arrows show the Culver Blvd. location of the former Hotel Playa, now the Dickinson and Gillespie headquarters (red arrow and pictured right), and the Sandwich Shoppe.

NAT AND META'S SHOPPE, PLAYA DEL REY, 1924. This photo, dated, 1924, of the sandwich, cold drinks and ice cream shop, was sponsored by local real estate promoters to feed their staff and visiting clients, (The original Playa Del Rey Shack?) They sold sodas for a nickel and ten-cent hot dogs. Note the Arrowhead Springs "charged water" tank in the forefront, and the old-timer resting on the stoop of the adjacent building. Thomas Ince would die mysteriously on William Randolph Heart's yacht this same year, and one time Playa Del Rey resident, Cecil B. Demille would acquire his studio land in Culver City.

Many years later, the location of the Sandwich Shoppe, now the intersection of Vista Del Mar and Culver Blvd., would be redeveloped several times. Long time residents might remember it as the location of Hickman's Chevron Station and Jake's on the Hill: a fabulous steak house that was a favorite with locals during the holidays and all through the year.

Thirty-One

Independence Day

If you were to travel to London Town, England, and take the time to look around, you would find at almost every corner and alley, plaques that commemorate the City's lush history. I think it is very important to know about the place where you live; and was very shocked to learn that in my corner of the World: Westchester/Playa Del Rey, California, very few people knew anything at all about it.

Someone once said, "Most people live on the world not in it." That may be true.

Having lived in many places; such as San Juan, Puerto Rico, New York, Seattle and St. Louis, I always made it my mission to learn about where I was. Not just the points on the compass, but learn about the history of the area; it's founders and before them; what was there before and what happened that created what was there now. A few years ago, I took upon myself to begin a new mission: writing a regular column for the Hometown News, with all but a few of the topics being the history of the "town." And rather than just writing about dry history, telling about it in little stories. I sure do hope you have enjoyed reading them as much as I have enjoyed writing them.

It is one of my favorite times of year again; Independence Day. We all will enjoy parades, cook-outs and perhaps fireworks, but most of all I hope that we remember the all of the people that have died to keep this country free. The US of A is on its' ear right now. The recession has hit us hard, and we remain embroiled in a protracted war; with many of our troops in harm's way. But I know that we will turn this country around, as we have always done, and are men and women will be home again soon, and back enjoying a summer bar-b-q with us.

Our area, formerly called Rancho La Ballona was suffering a great deal in the 1860's too. After the droughts of the 1860's decimated most of the rancho's cattle, squatters began to infest their huge land grant. During the first months of 1863, the smallpox epidemic raged all over Los Angeles, to such an extent that among the Indians, 90% perished, besides a great number of other people. Many Mexicans, chiefly of the impoverished classes, perished also, before the epidemic subsided, "for want of further material to work upon."

With the Civil War raging, July 4, 1863 was not celebrated in the city this year, but at the healthier environs of Camp Ballona harbor: now called Playa Del Rey, and more or less the location of Del Rey Lagoon. A few miles away, in what is now Culver City, a camp was established called Camp Latham, and commanded by Brigadier General George Wright. Wright was the Second Commander at Camp Latham, Rancho La Ballona. The Army patrolled the coastal area at what is now Playa Del Rey. In that year, 12 desertions occurred, as well as 3 deaths. It was believed that Confederates would launch an attack at Port Ballona, at the estuary of Ballona Creek. In California he commanded the largest force ever in the Far West; by 1862 he commanded 6,000 troops.

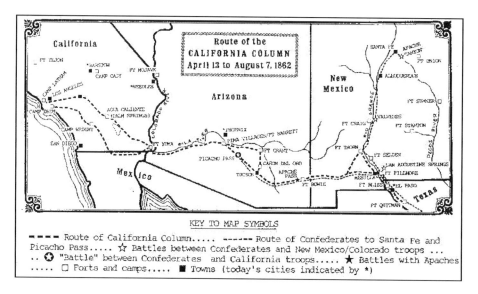

Camp Latham, Rancho La Ballona, was located on Ballona Creek in Rancho La Ballona at the present day intersections of Overland and Jefferson Boulevards. In 1862 the so-called *California Column* crossed from California into Arizona, New Mexico, and then Texas. Along the way the Californians fought the Battle of Picacho Pass and, afterward, the Battle of Apache Pass. The primary field commander was Colonel Christopher "Kit" Carson.

Wright later became Commander of the Department of the Pacific. On July 31 a detachment of troops from Drum barracks In San Pedro, encamped in the city to afford protection to the Unionists. Most of California was pro-Confederacy and a hotbed of spies from the South.

Regimental colors of the First and Second United States Cavalry, Camp Latham/ Rancho La Ballona, CA, commanded by Brig. General George Wright. After Wright became Commander of the Department of the Pacific, and while en route to his new command, he died at sea when his ship the Brother Jonathan sank off the California coast. His body was recovered six weeks later. He is interred in the Sacramento City Cemetery.

The camp was named for U.S. Senator Milton Latham, who as the sixth governor of California had the distinction of serving only five days before resigning in January 1860 to take the seat of Sen. David Broderick who had been killed the previous September in a pistol duel.

From a Civil War perspective it's interesting to note that Latham was a pro-southern democrat, and his election to the office of governor was opposed by those who feared that he would make California a pro-slavery state. He was succeeded by Lt. Gov. John Downey (and another pro-southern democrat), who became the state's first foreign-born governor (Ireland) and for whom the Southern California city of Downey is named.

Thirty-two

In nearby Hawthorne; the Beach Boys

Forty-six years ago this September, when the Beach Boys recorded, *Be True To Your School*, (September 2, 1963), the school they were referring to was probably Hawthorne High School.

Brian, Carl, Dennis Wilson and Al Jardine, all grew up a few miles from here and attended the school. Cousin Mike Love attended Dorsey High. Coincidentally, Olivia Trinidad Arias, who later became Olivia Harrison (George Harrison's wife), also attended and graduated in 1965.

The Beach Boys were at one time voted the most popular band in the world; ahead of the Beatles and the Rolling Stones, and many others. All this despite Brian Wilson receiving a failing grade in a Hawthorne High music class project, for submitting a song he had written.

Although only Dennis Wilson actually surfed regularly, the Beach Boys frequented the beaches of Playa Del Rey, a few miles up Imperial Highway from Hawthorne. Brian Wilson has regularly talked about his younger days at Gillis and Toe's Beach. Unfortunately, the original Wilson house where the Beach Boys grew up, and where they wrote and recorded many of their hit songs is gone. The house was demolished to make way for the 105 Freeway, and the musical history that went with it is remembered by a monument.

BEACH BOY MONUMENT.

The monument is located in the City of Hawthorne, between the Hawthorne Airport and the 105 Freeway. Get off the San Diego (405) Freeway on the El Segundo Blvd exit, and then take El Segundo Blvd east (about a mile and a half) to Prairie Avenue. Turn left (north) on Prairie, and go 4 1/2 blocks to 119th Street and turn right (east) on 119th. The monument is just two short blocks away, but 119th moves a bit to the left (north) when it passes Doty Ave., so remember to hang left on Doty to reconnect with 119th street a few yards to the north. The monument will be on your left (north) side, next to the freeway fence. So hop in your *Little Deuce Coupe* and come check it out.

*Completely useless factoid: The Pendleton shirts the Boys are wearing on the cover of the record was a last minute idea of Brian Wilson and Mike Love. Having secured a record contract with Capitol, they ran down to Del Amo Mall and purchased the shirts so they could create a uniform image for the photo shoot. I think they were purchased at Orbach's, a store chain that is no longer in business. Pendleton shirts were popular with South Bay surfers.

THE LOST BEACH BOY-David Marks (rt.), with Brian and Carl Wilson, Hawthorne High School.

No retelling of the Beach Boy saga, and their Hawthorne, California roots would be complete with David Marks. Sometimes referred to by Beach Boys historians as the "Lost" Beach Boy, Marks was part of the group's line-up when they signed with Capitol Records on July 16, 1962 - he played rhythm guitar and sang harmony vocals.

As a child, David had moved in across the street from the family home of the three Wilson brothers in 1956, and as the 50's progressed began singing and playing music with them on their family Sunday night sing-alongs. Inspired by seeing a 1958 performance by guitarist John Maus (later of the 60's hit-making group the Walker Brothers), David asked his parents to buy him a guitar. His wish came true on Christmas Eve, 1958. He began taking lessons from Maus (who had himself been a student of legendary early rocker Ritchie Valens) almost at once. In 1959, David Marks and Carl Wilson had begun to develop their own style of playing electric guitar (David having introduced Maus to Carl, they both had the same teacher.) Brian eventually realized that the combination of Carl and David could bring a rock guitar sound to his original compositions, and the two then-teenagers were participants in Brian's first songwriting efforts that led to the later hit single Surfer Girl.

After a long hiatus, Marks is again playing with some of the Beach Boy off-shoot bands.

Thirty-three

Halloween

What better time to read a book by Stephen King: Maine's King of Horror, than at Halloween, when our minds turn to "ghoulies and ghosties, and long legged beasties and things that go bump in the night"? Make no bones about it; Stephen King can scare the Wella hair color right out of your curls. So to get into the Halloween mood, why not give yourself a good scare with one of his terrifying novels, ideally suited for the creepy Halloween season? And try my favorite: Pet Semetary. Or, if you want to save the price of the book or movie; or you don't have a library card, I can show you a place that will give you the willies—right here in your own backyard.

The root of the word *Halloween*, and the term *Hallowed ground*, of course share the word: *hallow*, a word usually used as a verb, meaning "to make holy or sacred, to sanctify or consecrate, to venerate." It generally refers to places like cemeteries, churchyards, and historical sites: places where for instance, throughout the ages and at every corner of the world, coronations were held for great Kings. In a Gothic sense, the word means simply: *holy*. And *hallows* can refer to saints, the relics (including remains) of the saints, the relics of gods, or shrines in which relics are kept.

Of course you probably know the plot of King's book involves a pet *cemetery*: built beside a desecrated Indian burial ground-- it has the power to bring back the dead. So speaking of desecrated burial grounds, you needn't travel back to Maine's Aroostook County to find one, as we have our own cemetery right here in good ol' Playa Vista, CA. And on Halloween night, while you are taking the kids out for tricks and treats; particularly if you are near The Bluffs , and as you roam the streets, and the moon-lit fog and mists roll in-- maybe listen for the drum of a distant tom-tom or look for a loin cloth clad specter in search of his severed head. Because right in our own backyard, we have desecrated a cemetery; or at least that is what local Indian tribal members say—digging up ancient remains of Tongvan tribe members—from *their* hallowed ground. It was bad enough to dig them up, but then, we placed them in paint buckets—one rib and one skull at a time, and stored the whole lot of them—some say as many as 400 Native Americans, in storage trailers—kind of like a mobile home or motel for bones and artifacts. Spooky, huh? But just remember: *"You can check-in, but you can never leave."* Well, at least three years later they haven't.

The Tongva, later renamed Gabrielino's by the Europeans, were the original settlers of this area. There was as many as thirty-one Gabrielino villages (at the time of the first Spanish land expedition) within a mile of known courses of the Los Angeles River—now called Ballona Creek or The Wetlands in our area. The Gabrielino were known to roam widely in their search for food but always gravitated to sites for their villages mainly because of the location of water sources. But while the Gabrielino understood the importance of water to their survival, they were also aware of the dangers of the river, having experienced the occasional flooding that threatened their homes. For this reason, the natives settled on higher ground at a sufficient distance from the river, and the sea, to ensure their safety during time of flood. One of these settlements was on The Bluffs of Westchester and Playa Del Rey; as they knew the lower lands were uninhabitable, and only gathered, hunted and fished there.

An early1800's European interpretation of a Tongvan village. Tongvan means, "People of the Earth."

So when in 2004, an Indian cemetery was unearthed on the up-slope of The Bluffs, it was determined that the law governing these sorts of things, enacted in 1872, did not cover this kind of historical find--as the graves were many centuries or thousands of years older. So it was over to Gerald's Hardware Store, or someplace, for a whole bunch of large white pails—and they were scooped up; rib by rib and jawbone by jawbone--tossed in a can and put into storage. All entities involved in the alleged destruction of the graves were aware that the area was inhabited by the Gabrielino/Tongva people and that the site in question was known to be the site of the ancient village—now our village, of *Saa'anga*; later called "Guaspet" by the Spanish. Everyone knew it was there and it was documented for many years. And if this had been a non-Indigenous cemetery, neither the local, neither state, nor federal governments would have allowed the destruction of the property or the ongoing construction; and they certainly would not have allowed the disturbance of human remains or the removal of funerary objects from the graves.

"What you have here are several different eras of burial grounds in one area," said Johntommy Rosas, the vice-chairman of one of the bands of Gabrielino Tongva. Photo: Construction workers fill buckets with skulls, and ribs and funerary objects. Archeologists were called in later.

But we still don't know what will be the ultimate fate of these once great people, as court battles continue to rage—as does the building and construction.

So again, as you take the kids out on Halloween night, and pass near The Bluffs on that full moon night, hold on tightly to their <u>hands.</u> There may be someone out there—searching for one. And if you live in Playa Vista; when you take the garbage out at night, make sure you put the lid on-- nice and tight. And whatever you do, don't let the dog dig for bones in the backyard.

Happy Halloween!

Thirty-four

"Duke…why don't you quit your complaining and start coming up with some solutions?"

OK! What I would like to see in Westchester, Playa Del Rey….

1. **A Westchester/Playa Del Rey Trolley System**: This could begin with "rubber wheeled" trackless trolleys, as Fresno and Monterey, CA have done. The routes would go between these points: **Loyola Marymount University**: both the Loyola Blvd. and LMU Drive gates, **Ralph's Grocery** on Lincoln Boulevard, Jefferson and Lincoln, **Howard Hughes Center**, Sepulveda and Manchester Boulevards, and Culver and Vista Del Mar in Playa Del Rey. The routes would take more passenger cars off the roads, and run a loop-line past some of the most popular spots in town: Lincoln Boulevard, Playa Del Rey, Howard Hughes Center, and **Downtown Westchester**. These are 20-30 passenger trolleys, burn natural gas and come delivered with AC and heaters. For $1.00; .50 for Seniors/students with valid I.D./kids under 12, you could ride the route anytime—round-trip, and hail the trolley at any corner along the routes: Lincoln, Sepulveda, 80th and Manchester. The *"TURN-A-ROUNDS"* would be at Howard Hughes Center, Del Rey Lagoon, and Ralph's Grocery/**El Dorado Bowl** parking lot. It's no coincidence, or course, that these spots are active stops for regular local and long distance METRO and other scheduled bus service, "feeding" longer distance commuters. *Sumitomo Light Rail and Geofocus*, who built the electric cars for the Blue and Green lines of Los Angeles METRO, have the logistics infrastructure in place to make this happen, (pardon the shameless, self-serving plug).

   I call it; *D.R.R.A.T.*; **Del Rey Rapid Area Transit.** During summer months, we could run two additional *"SURF"* routes; running seasonal "spurs" down Vista Del Mar to Highland, and another extending to Marina Del Rey: stopping at both **The Waterside at Marina del Rey** and **Fisherman's' Village**. Cars could be wheel chair friendly, and sport bike, surf board, fishing pole, and golf club racks, and recycling/trash bins. Imagine your children simply going to a corner and hailing a trolley; or LMU students utilizing these trolleys to shop at local markets, Playa Vista, travel to local dining spots, or riding up and down the hill to see a movie at **The Bridge**? I could have this up and running in 90 days, and profitable in six months.

Modern clean running *NGV* Trolleys are relieving traffic congestion and pollution all over the country; in fact all over the world. And although riders prefer electric trolleys on tracks, this solution is well received at hundreds of communities. Visitors could also park their cars, at Howard Hughes Center, for instance, and ride the trolleys and experience the richness of this area. There are no "stations," just hail a trolley as they pass by!

Advertising on the sides of the trolleys and with inside video presentations, could cover much of the operating costs. Rather than just sitting around in traffic, and burning gas, wouldn't you take a trolley with a group of friends for a Saturday night dinner to **Allejo's** on Lincoln, **Pancho's** on Highland, or **Salerno Beach Restaurant** on Vista Del Mar? Maybe ride it to the park to play tennis? Or send the kids to **Westchester Golf Course** or down to surf El Porto? Special "Party Trolleys" could be chartered for pizza parties to **Tower Pizza**, home tour events, parades and Christmas light/firework show/boat parade viewing; or to attend local concerts at Playa Vista and Burton Chace Park. **Custom Hotel** visitors would gain access to town as well. Many of these routes pass right by, or near local churches and houses of worship as well. Internet enabled computers or hand held pda's and cell phones, could track the location of the nearest trolley at any time. By the way, kids could take these to school and back too; and I would bet that many local merchants would validate and refund the cost of the trolley with a minimum purchase.

2. **Westchester/Playa Del Rey Community Gardens**; at 80th an Emerson, and **Westchester High School**, there are two areas of fallow land that would be ideal. I call it: **Walden Farms**. Behind **Orville Wright Junior High School** and Westchester High School, we could invite people to plant a few feet of their favorite vegetables. Come to think of it, you could grab your seeds and take a trolley to the spots! At harvest, local growers could trade their bounty with other growers, sending everyone home with a fresh salad bowl; or fresh fruits for drying and preserving. Many folks would love to grow their own vegetables; or fresh flowers, but lack the land on their own property to do so. And this is great for apartment dwellers that have no land at all. The Westchester High School property even has unused and soon to be demolished green houses!

3. **Trout Fishing at the Wetlands of Playa Del Rey and Del Rey Lagoon**: For centuries, local wetlands and the former Los Angeles River; now Ballona Creek, were teaming with brown and speckled trout, steelhead, minnows and catfish. Reintroducing these local species would help rebuild our local ecology, and create a great fishing spot. Anglers wouldn't have to drive to the Sierras to catch a mess of fresh fish either, and yep, you guessed it; you could take a trolley car.

Along with Lagoon fishing, the Del Rey Wetland areas are ideal for reintroducing local species. Trails could be built to minimize damage to any or the fragile areas, and LAPD bicycle officers could patrol the region. Cleverly camouflaged *Andy Gumps*, recycling and trash-cans could be installed to minimize litter.

4. **The Dunes Bicycle and Skate Trails:** Off-road bikers and even skateboarders would love to ride the trails and former streets of Playa Del Rey and Surfridge. Roller bladers' might

like it too. An extension of the bike trail could be built through the property; with a relatively cheap underpass being built under Vista Del Mar. Bikes don't create pollution of course, and relatively little, if any impact would be made to the **El Segundo Blue Butterfly Preserve**.

Off-road bicyclists and skateboarders would love the chance to conquer the former streets and trails of Playa Del Rey. Joggers might like to run along the dunes as well.

5. **Westchester Golf Course-RE-DESIGN:** O.K. **L.A.W.A.**, enough is enough! Just pop a hole in the fence near the existing 14th tee, and give us back the 3 holes you took from us. Run the fairways east towards the new Fire Station. My buddies and I could have this done in 90 days too. Let's quit all the talk about environmental impact studies. It was zoned for a golf course, and that's exactly what it is. Us golfers, and for that matter, the residents, are sick of all the hooey.

> *"Millions of men have lived to fight, build palaces and boundaries, shape destinies and societies; but the compelling force of all times has been the force of originality and creation profoundly affecting the roots of human spirit."—Ansel Adams*

6. **A Westchester ANTIQUE AND COLLECTOR FAIR:** Held on the last Sunday of every month, and located at the picnic area of Westchester Park, a monthly festival would be held for antiquers' and collectors. NOT A SWAPMEET! There is plenty of parking in the Library parking lot, or you could ride your bike or walk to it. Merchants along Manchester and Lincoln Boulevard would benefit from the additional patrons as well. I spoke to my friend, artist and musician Steve O'Loughlin, and he and his Irish band would love to play on the opening day. Perhaps a local restaurant or caterer could bar-b-q and sell refreshments.

7. **A TONGVA/Gabrielino Native American Information Center-**We should celebrate the original habitants of this area and their rich culture with an **Interprative Center** near *The Bluffs*; which the Tongva called: *Saa'anga*. Santa Fe Springs, CA has built a very fine one, right in the middle of their former oil fields—a former Tongva Village. I have already written the **William Hannon Foundation** and **Fritz Burns Foundation**, asking for their financial support to this worthwhile educational endeavor. And I would hope that local developers, Cattelus **(Prologis)** and **Playa Vista Corporation** might chip in; and chip in the land and parking area that would be needed.

At Heritage Park, in Santa Fe Springs, tours are held every day at the Tongva Exhibit.
This exhibit celebrates the culture of the Tongva people who lived in this area for thousands of years. Their dwellings, known as kiches (above), were domed-shaped structures made of willow and tule reeds. This exhibit features the structures, tools and plant material essential to their life. Local school children should know this part of The Westchester Bluffs local history.
http://www.santafesprings.org/library/heritage/tongva.asp

The great photographer and naturalist Ansel Adams once said, *"Millions of men have lived to fight, build palaces and boundaries, shape destinies and societies; but the compelling force of all times has been the force of originality and creation profoundly affecting the roots of human spirit."*

I think it is long past the time to start thinking outside the box, and to begin finding solutions that are original and can help re-shape the destiny of our fair corner of the world; Westchester/Playa Del Rey. These are just a few ideas—I am just getting warmed up.

Millions of men have lived to fight... and it only takes a few of us to <u>start</u> the fight.

Thirty-five

What is going on with Lincoln Boulevard!? Let's talk about another road first.

I returned again to Westchester for a brief time, after many months spent on the road-part of that time as John Steinbeck called her- on *The Mother Road*. Although only nostalgic sections of it remain, *Route 66* was the probable westerly route taken by many of our parents when they moved to this area. With a water bag hanging from their automobile hood ornaments, a few bucks in their pockets, and a cooler full of iced Coca-Cola and sandwiches, many young married couples jumped off at places like Chicago and St. Louis, and headed west to this amazing and bountiful area-the end of the road being our neighbor to the north-Santa Monica, ending at Olympic and Lincoln Boulevards.

It was the same path taken by many of us on family vacations, back to places like Albuquerque, Springfield, Joplin, Carthage, and Chicago. I was fortunate enough to travel the road twice-the first time about 45 years ago, in true family style: station wagon, rented roof rack-fighting the whole long way with siblings for elbow room. But my memory of this first trip on Route 66 is void of any recollection of those battles, and full of memories of treacherous desert crossings at midnight (tire blow-outs and gully washers), unfinished dirt and gravel sections of the highway, clean well kept Southwestern and Midwestern towns, Mule Trading Posts, Stuckey's, White Castle's, roadside motels, dinosaurs, tee-pees, and countless nameless coffee shops and ice stops.

Always beginning on a summer Friday night at 8PM, the first leg of the journey was a wild, near non-stop sleigh ride from Westchester to Gallup, NM. You HAD to cross the Mohave at night in those days, as air conditioning was a real rarity-and August the deserts hottest month. You would stop for gas in Needles, CA, and take a deep breath and stretch your legs,-knowing you made it. One could not help but think what it must have been like, less than 100 years before, to make the same trip on horseback or Conestoga wagon. Of course, a 2000 mile trip by air is a three or four hours for most of us now.

So here I was, in places like Tulsa, OK, Springfield, Bourbon and St Louis, MO, driving again on the same roads that brought my parents to Westchester-and me to my Fathers parents in Benton Harbor, MI, and it was as if time had stopped, as certain sections of the road are meticulously maintained in pure 1950's era- signs, buildings, soda fountains, gas stations and motels. There is even a (I think *the* last) Mule Trading Post in Rolla, MO, but I could not bear to stop and see it, fearful that it had changed. These trading posts were the places that sold real Indian: jewelry, arrowheads, basket ware, moccasins, bull-whips, spears and tomahawks-all fascinating items for any young child. At one point, there were dozens of them scattered along the road that traverses the Ozark Mountains-steeped in history, with places named for people like, Lewis, Clark, Boone and Jefferson.

US 66 was officially decommissioned (that is, officially removed from the United States Highway System) on June 27, 1985 after it was decided the route was no longer relevant and had been replaced by the Interstate Highway System. Portions of the road that passed through Illinois, Missouri, New Mexico, and Arizona have been designated a National Scenic Byway of the name "Historic Route 66". It has begun to return to maps in this form. But rather than destroy this fascinating and historic section of Middle-America, our Midwestern cousins have preserved and protected it, and its' road side attractions. You can still: G*et Your Kicks on Route 66*. It is organized and orderly-and seldom hokey.

This brings me back to another National Scenic Byway, and an All-American Road- Lincoln Boulevard, Westchester, CA USA-also known as Highway 1.

Now I know I can be, and most probably am, a silly nostalgic. Webster's defines a nostalgic as: *"a wistful or excessively sentimental person, yearning for a return to or of some past period or irrecoverable condition."* But I would like to think of myself as a practical nostalgic. In other words, I realize some change must occur, but change without proper planning produces useful results. It can be the proverbial fork-in-the-road, and it is why God invented maps in the first place. And I know, just as you can't un-muddy the water after you've played in it, or re-wrap a Christmas gift-you can't go back.

You should proceed however, using what you have learned along the road, and put that to practical use. And having said that, you do not have to be a road engineer or world traveler or master of anything, to realize that what is occurring, between LAX-Manchester Parkway and Jefferson Boulevards, is a harmful, ill conceived aberration, which will forever change the tradition and landscape of our little part of heaven-Westchester/Playa Del Rey. It has been changed not to benefit the local residents, but to accommodate those commuters and travelers who choose to use the road as an alternative to the San Diego Freeway-most of whom do not stop in town, shop in town, or benefit it's merchants in any way- and do not even know the name of this town.

Just last week, it took me the same time to drive from LAX to 83rd Street, that it took me only a few days before to drive a meandering mountain road, from Branson Landing, MO to Springfield, MO-about 43 miles-in about 45 minutes. And as we continue to build new homes, condominiums and apartments in and around the area, it will only get worse. Our neighborhoods are finally surrounded on all sides, by what is arguably to most congested roads and freeways in the world, and we continue to "densify" the region without proper thought to infrastructure. For instance, besides traffic, the condition of our public schools is a travesty, and the parking situation at most of our shopping centers and eateries is downright crumby-not to mention the air quality and noise pollution that we now suffer with. And don't get me started again on our beaches!

In July, Councilman Bill Rosendahl met with community members and mass transit advocates, to develop plans to spend accumulated traffic mitigation funds, including Lincoln Boulevard, which can only be spent in Rosendahl's coastal district. His plan includes developing a rail line down Lincoln Boulevard! Did he ever hear about the demise of the Los Angeles "Red-Cars?" Been there-done that.

Un-congested drives on Lincoln Boulevard have gone the way of the Burma Shave sign.

So I am getting ready to head east and down south again, because this is what I do for a living. I am looking forward to Iowa corn fed steak dinners, Tennessee deep-fried pickles, Kansas City bar-b-q, and to people who still smile when they refill your coffee cup. It's a little bit slower, I'll admit, but when faced with this local alternative, I will find a way to somehow blend in. Even if I still wear Aloha shirts on Saturday nights and listen to the Beach Boys, and dream at night of the ones dear to and apart from me, sunny days and the great warm-water- spring-swells that used to grace our beaches.

"We cannot continue to band-aid the traffic problems in this City," Rosendahl
said. "Our transportation infrastructure is a real problem that calls for vision, for
bold thinking and long-range planning."-*Los Angeles County Bicycle Coalition*

The Midwest is a place where people are known for their quiet but frank style, and when they get hosed, they are not afraid to object to it and give you a piece of their mind. So make no mistake, the combined unstoppable forces of LAX and a few unscrupulous developers are hosing us all-and we just fall in line for our daily Soylent ration.

Just remember that many of your folks motored out on Route 66, to create a better, less congested place for their families-and not for us to inherit this desperate situation.

And yes, I fear that this is an irrecoverable condition.

Thirty-six

Thanksgiving

It's Thanksgiving again—another one of those times when we should reflect upon all that we have to be thankful for. And another year has almost passed in the blink of an eye. Even here, the season is changing.

Baseball is over—at least for our teams, and I look forward to reading the winter updates on those players the Los Angeles Dodgers acquire. It sure was a tough season. We could use a few more *bats;* local Bellflower boy, Jeff Kent, can't carry the team alone. Another local guy, Whittier's' Garciaparra may not make it to Vero Beach—Nomo Nomar? But the *Bums,* despite a fourth place finish, thankfully still managed to play.500 ball.

The end of the season is sad time for me for many reasons. It's good to listen to games on the way home from work—it makes the commute bearable. We also watch all the games, and as I don't follow pro football; the television set is now open season for my daughter. If I see another *Hannah Montana* program again, I will eat the remote control. Of all the things I am thankful for, *TiVo* is not one of them.

This year marked the 40th anniversary of my last game at International Little League; now Westchester Little League. In 1967, we played all of our games at Diamond 3, Westchester Park, as we had lost our field to a train trestle and road widening on Aviation Boulevard in 1964—and that was some field too. At Westchester Park, we didn't have an outfield fence. Instead there were orange traffic cones marking the 200 feet to center, and to 185 feet to right and left fields. One of the Dads, Mr. Rowe, had burned holes in the grass with gasoline at the measured spots you were to place the cones. I know I have said it before, but a Little League program without a real field is like a combination plate without the tacos. But we got by. And this was before the north runway, and you could still hear yourself think at the park.

My very last game there, was for the Championship; the Giants vs. my team, the Cardinals. We had won the regular season that year, but the Giants were dominating the playoffs. We had to fight back, the whole long way through the losers' bracket to get back into it. The star of the Giants that year was a hard throwing southpaw; Rick "Fitz" Fitzgerald. He could really bring on the heat. I was the starting pitcher of that game against *Fitz*; and my little brother Kevin, the starting catcher.

Now I should go down in the annals of Westchester Little League as the best starting pitcher in the league; for 1 inning. A catcher, I relieved a few games; often for none other than my own brother, Kevin, who was the only one on the team with the guts to catch me. I hit plenty more batters than ever hit me. After striking out the first two batters however; all fastballs, I threw a wild pitch which skipped up and broke my brothers' hand. He was taken to the dugout and then to the hospital and a new pitcher was called in and I put the equipment on. Kevin actually made it back to the end of the game. You can imagine how bad I felt for him. I mean; I was really miserable, but we had a game to play.

Fitz was really bringing it that day, and after 5 innings, the score was 1-0 Giants. The only run was unearned, but Fitz must have struck out 14 batters at this point. In the bottom of the last inning, with two out, Tommy Nye beat out an infield single, and was jumping up and down on the bag and yelling all sorts of stuff when I came to bat. You won't believe it, but this was the exact time that my Mother brought my brother back from the hospital. From the batter's box I saw the cast on his right arm; he is right handed. The Cardinal fans were all standing and screaming like nuts, but quieted down when I went 0 and 2 on two high fast balls. All the pitchers in the league knew I was a sucker for the *high cheese*, and I missed those first two pitches by a mile. I fouled off the next 11 pitches; no kidding. I figured I was going down; but not without a fight.

Fitz wound up and threw a low sinker; but it didn't sink, and I creamed it. The ball must have hung in the air for 45 minutes, because I think Tommy Nye had already crossed home plate and was putting mustard on his hot dog when, per the home plate umpire, the ball bounced *"inches in front of the right-center field cones; and past them."* Ruling: a ground rule double. No free steak dinner for me; or for Fitz, as I just broke up his no hitter. My coach, Dave Houghton was as mad as any human ever was, but his argument was useless. It was a double, and Tommy Nye was ordered back to third base, and I was sent back to second. The next batter up, batting in my brothers spot; struck out, and the 1967 Cardinal season was over. We got our trophies and went on to our summer jobs, and wonderful days on the beach. Later that year, at Christmastime, I got my first real job; selling Christmas trees at Royal Market in Culver City.

Two years later, from the Visitation School 1969 graduation class photo- Fitzgerald, far right: second row. That's yours truly on the end: second row left. PHOTO: First row left, Gerry Street—who recently sent this to me. Gerry's' father, long time Westchester resident, Colonel Bruce Street, was Chief of Staff to General Douglas MacArthur, and recently passed away—many of us from this same class still say in touch and attended the services at Holy Cross Cemetery.

I am very thankful for those days and for this town and for all the wonderful people it had and has in it. The seasons come and go; as do some of those people, but baseball remains an ongoing barograph; marking the first pure days of spring and the waning autumn months; as the days shorten and the nights become cooler. Winter is just a time to oil your glove and wait for spring.

In 1967, The Los Angeles Dodgers finished in eighth place, and at "Bat Day" at Dodger Stadium, I got an (Inglewood/Playa del Rey's own) Jimmy Lefebvre bat. My brother Kevin got a Bob Bailey bat. Tom Nye got a Ron Fairly. Harmon Killebrew and Carl Yastrzemski (AL) tied the home run leader list with a clean and respectable 44 home runs-- Hank Aaron (NL) hit 37. Roberto Clemente hit .357; winning his last batting title. Incidentally, hometown boy Lefebvre is managing the 2008 Chinese Olympic baseball team. I am sure many of you remember that his father coached the St Bernard's Varsity baseball team, and that his dear mother ran the girls P.E. program. There is a lot of history in this town and a lot more to write about.

And you know? This can be a pretty fine town, when people are willing to step up to the plate and fight off those inside pitches. If you stop fighting, you might as well stop breathing.

So a very Happy Thanksgiving to all of you; and Fitz—where ever you are, God bless you, and thanks for some great times. You were a great pitcher, but Buddy--that *was* a homer—and 40 years later; I am not one bit sorry about your steak.

Thirty-seven

The Mighty Men of Del Rey-Loyola University Football

On November 28th, we'll all be sitting around the television watching (probably) USC defeat the UCLA Bruins. I am growing used to it. This is of course the biggest rivalry in Los Angeles College Football, but in the 1930's, Westchester; then called Playa Del Rey, was also involved in a college football rivalry.

In those days the Loyola Football team; The Loyola University of Los Angeles' Lions, competed as an independent against teams from the Pacific Coast Conference and the Pacific Coast Intercollegiate Conference(1921-1951).

Coached by ex-Notre Dame Assistant and Line Coach, Tom Lieb, Loyola fielded an impressive squad throughout the 1930's. Playing UCLA in 1934, Coach Lieb was very familiar with his opponent. The Bruins were coached by Bill Spaulding, who Lieb had competed against while coaching Notre Dame, and Spaulding at Kalamazoo, and later while at Wisconsin, while Spaulding was coaching Minnesota. Loyola also competed against UCLA in baseball, track and hockey. Lieb also coached the Loyola Lion Hockey Team.

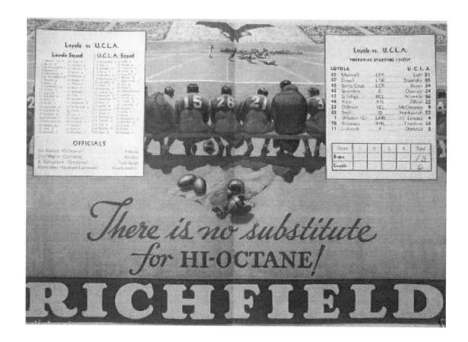

Scorecard, Loyola University vs. UCLA, November 29, 1934. The Bruins defeated the Lions, 13-6.

The 1934 match was played on a Thursday for some reason, although college football did regularly stage games on Fridays. The game was probably carried on radio, but the radio logs of the Los Angeles Times for that day make no mention of it. On the other hand, the following year, the 1935 match between Loyola and UCLA, played at 2PM on November 23, 1935, was carried on radio by KFI, KFWB, KNX, and KFAC.

Incidentally, on that same day in 1935, it appears that KNX was the only L.A. station that was broadcasting the 10th annual USC-Notre Dame Game from South Bend, Indiana at 11:30 a.m. USC lost the game 20-13.

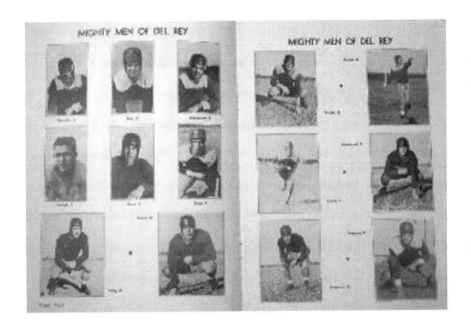

The Mighty Men of Del Rey; the 1934 Loyola Lion Football squad. Westchester had not been named yet, and most folks referred to the Jesuit campus as Playa Del Rey, Venice or just "Loyola".

The Loyola Marching Band, Gilmore Stadium, 1935. The **Loyola** .Band was a **major attraction** for years at **Gilmore Stadium**, the **Los Angeles Coliseum**, and the **Pasadena Rose Bowl**.

Many of the Loyola Football games were played at Gilmore Stadium near Fairfax, Cursen Street and Beverly Boulevard. That year, another Los Angeles landmark opened close by, the Original Farmers Market.

Finally, did you know that 16 Lions made it to the National Football League? They were; Bob Boyd, Gene Brito, Ernis Cheathem, Jack Dwyer, Earl Elsey, Neil Ferris, Hal Giancanelli, Frank Hrabetin, Don Klosterman(The Duke of Del Rey), Dick Moje, Maury Nipp, Vince Pacewic, Al Pollard, Eddie Saenz, Carroll Vogelear, and Bob Wilkinson.

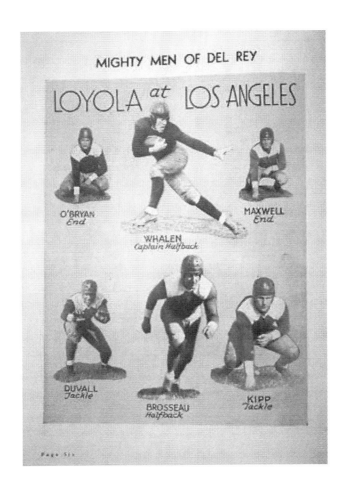

Fight on Lions!

Thirty-eight

Speaking of Beaches? How was Gillis Beach named?

Robert Conran Gillis

At the turn of the century (1900) Los Angeles remained a somewhat sleepy little brother to San Francisco. The population of the town was a mere 102,479, of which 4,900 listed their occupation as "real estate promoter," and there were just 72 LAPD Officers. There had been a Gold Rush in the north, but now the rush was on for land in the south. In what is now Santa Monica, Colonel Robert S. Baker, founder of Bakersfield, wanted to build a new town called Truxton- named after a Revolutionary War era hero, Commodore, Thomas Truxton. He developed parts of "Santa Monica" instead, named for a spring.

Another real estate developer was Robert Conran Gillis. Although best known for developing, and probably saving the Pacific Palisades, R. C. Gillis, and his company The Santa Monica Land and Water Company (see, Chinatown, 1974-The California Water Wars) was almost single-handedly responsible for developing most of Santa Monica, Pacific Palisades, West LA, (Sawtelle) and Playa Del Rey.

One time owner of the Santa Monica Evening Outlook, Gillis, a Canadian immigrant, possessed an uncanny eye for valuable real estate ventures. His own home, at 406 Adelaide St. Santa Monica, is a historic landmark, and remains one of the most coveted addresses in the area. The street is named for Gillis' daughter.

R.C. Gillis House, 406 Adelaide Drive. Craftsman residence built- 1906-1910.
Today, actor Jeff "Wild Bill Hickok" Bridges lives next door.

Abbot Kinney, of Venice Beach fame, was the first developer of Pacific Palisades, although only the eucalyptus trees that he had planted there remain- the only testament to his vision. He mistakenly planted the resin-rich trees to sell as firewood. After going broke, and selling the land to Collis Huntington (uncle of Henry Huntington), who dreamed of a deep water port in Santa Monica Bay, development began at a fever pace.

Huntington built a wharf extending 4,720 feet out into the ocean off Potrero Canyon, which during its first year of operation handled more than 300 vessels. All that is left today of this effort is a plaque marking the piers original location.

When the decision was made to establish the port of Los Angeles at San Pedro, not in Santa Monica, and with the death of Huntington, his heirs eventually sold the entire 226 acres in 1926 to Gillis. Gillis was President of the Santa Monica Land and Water Company, whose large-scale land purchases set the pattern for subdivisions from Westwood to Pacific Palisades in the early 1900s, and he was always searching for land.

The Sisters of St. Joseph of Carondelet were also searching- for a site for Mount St. Mary's College. But Gillis and the Pacific Palisades founders 'Methodists all' scotched the plan and the college was eventually built in what is now Bundy Canyon, in Brentwood.
Also in 1926, vaudeville star Will Rogers bought his first piece of beach property for $977,372. Gillis arranged for the sale of 2,000 feet of beach frontage at the mouth of Santa Monica Canyon that belonged to the Pacific Land Corporation and the Pacific Palisades Association, which had both fallen on hard times. At the time a string of newly built beach clubs lined the sand from Santa Monica to the Palisades. Rogers developed his ranch in the canyon above, which was frequented by cowboy actors Tom Mix and William S. Hart (both would sadly became pallbearers for Rogers) and of all people, gunslinger Marshall Wyatt Earp, who had moved to California, and all of whom were regularly entertained by Gillis at his Santa Monica

Beach House, not far from present Will Rogers State Beach.

Next came Playa Del Rey. The subdivider was The Beach Land Company, Henry P. Barbour, president. Associated with Barbour were R. C. Gillis, F. H. Rindge (also a street name), M. H. Sherman, E. P. Clark, E. T. Earl, Arthur Fleming, A. I. Smith and P. M. Green. This Company had acquired from Louis and Joseph Mesmer nearly all of the town of Port Ballona and adjoining property. It gave a sixty-foot right of way to The Los Angeles-Hermosa Beach & Redondo Railway.

And so the town of Playa Del Rey was born, and with that, a street and beach named for Robert Conran "Gillis." This was a very "happening" beach for many years.

R.C. Gillis Beach House, 1267-1301 Palisades Beach Road- built 1923.

Beach volleyball and windsurfing were both invented in the area (though predecessors were invented in some form by Duke Kahanamoku in Hawaii). Venice, Kinneys' Dream, also known as Dogtown, is credited with being the birthplace of skateboarding and the place where Rollerblading first became popular. Area beaches are popular with surfers, and one beach, Dockweiler Beach, being moved from Gillis and Toes Beach, hosts the 36th Annual Gillis Volleyball Tournament, this August 12th and 13th. Info @thegillis.com.

For most, the once bustling Gillis Beach, with it's' "oasis," is just a stop on the bike path now. And Gillis Street- is the last lonely, and almost forgotten street in Playa Del Rey.

Thirty-nine

The Playa Del Rey Incline Railroad

THE LAGOON LINE, JUST SOUTH OF VISTA DEL MAR AND CULVER BOULEVARDS, AND THE PLAYA DEL REY INCLINE Railroad, 1907.

Venice passengers joined at its junction with the Redondo Line. A short walk south brought you to the famous cable , or "Funicular" railway, whose cars, "Alphonse" and "Gaston", carried visitors up the steep palisades to the subdivision laid out on top, between 1901 and 1908.

The Lagoon Line was traversed regularly by the Balloon Route Trolley Trip cars which paused for lunch at the wooden pavilion at Playa del Rey.

Forty

The birth of the Shelby Mustang at Westchester, California

One of my favorite themes has been the history of auto racing on the Westside of Los Angeles.

This bygone era began with the first ever board track at Playa Del Rey, and later the massive Mines Field Raceway at what is now LAX and Westchester. Racetracks operated all over Los Angeles; from Beverly Hills to Carson.

Mines Field Raceways' B shaped 1.9 mile dirt road course was opened in 1932, and closed in 1936. A shorter 1.56 dirt road course was used in 1934, hosting an AAA champ car race. Much of the area is now LAX/Westchester.

Of course many changes occurred in the area, but it seems fitting that Carol Shelby would choose Westchester to move his Shelby Mustang plant. Street racing aficionados will remember that Westchester was the home of the last true hand built (modified) Ford Shelby Mustangs and Cobra Mustangs-all built by racing great Carol Shelby's company at a then abandoned LAX aircraft hangar at 6501 Imperial Highway. I can remember these being "test driven" all over town; and at breakneck speeds on Pershing Drive. The first Ford Mustangs were introduced at the New York World's Fair on April 17, 1964 to rave reviews. Shelby began modifying them shortly thereafter.

Carol Shelby, at his Venice, CA shop in an AC Cobra, 1963,(left). At LAX a 1965 Shelby Mustang GT; the engine was a modified K-code 289ci Windsor V8 with special "Cobra" valve covers, tri-Y headers, a special intake manifold and Holley carburetor increasing power from 271 to 325 hp. All original cars were painted "Wimbledon White."

Moving his plant, only a few years before from 1042 Princeton Drive in Venice, and at the urging of Lee Iacocca, Shelby began production of the hugely successful Shelby Mustangs in 1964. He continued to build the cars in Westchester until LAX evicted him in 1966. You can view a classic TV commercial of the Mustangs(1967's) being driven along the LAX runway at : http://www.youtube.com/watch?v=fYD8w-nP89s The Theme Building is in the background. From there, the cars were made at a Ford plant in Michigan; basically becoming a production car. In 2006 Ford introduced the new Shelby Mustang; made in Las Vegas, NV.

Large aircraft hangers were leased from North American Aviation at LAX in Westchester on January 1, 1965 for $8,800.00 per month. Shelby American, Inc., sold the new Shelby Mustang GT350 for about $4500.00. My grandfather, William "Lloyd" Thompson, retired Ford Motor Company employee/ Detroit, MI, worked at the plant.

And with Playa Del Rey being the birthplace of board-auto racing, and Westchester the home of Mines Field Raceway and Shelby American, not even a plaque or memorial reminds of us of these racing pioneers and these locations; born along, and forgotten near, the bluffs and foggy dunes of Westchester/Playa Del Rey.

Forty-one

Little Green Men in Space Ships at Playa Del Rey

Considering our proximity to LAX and the old Hughes Aircraft runway, Westchester has been the sightings of hundreds of Unidentified Flying Objects; most of them off-course approaching aircraft, and sometimes experimental craft from Hughes. Additionally, the skies above us are regularly graced with various missile launchings from nearby Point Magu Naval Air Station, just north of us.

Playa Del Rey was also the site of the filming of "Earth vs. The Flying Saucers" in 1956. Most of the filming occurred near the Los Angeles Hyperion at Vista Del Mar and Imperial Highway, but the cast, many dressed in spacesuits frequented local coffee shops and restaurants, much to the joy of local residents.

Earth vs. The Flying Saucers is set in 1956, a year before the first satellite, Sputnik I went into orbit. In the film, "Project Skyhook," a U.S. effort to launch a dozen satellites, is visited by a flying saucer. The sand dunes of Playa Del Rey proved a great landing area for the filming.

The year after film premiered, a rash of UFO sightings occurred all over California, and several eye witnesses claimed they were visited by extraterrestrials. A strange story about stalled cars and little men was told to authorities and the press on the morning of November 6, 1957, when Richard Kehoe, an employee of the General Telephone Company of Santa Monica, related his early-morning experience.

Kehoe claimed that while driving along Vista del Mar at Playa del Rey in California at 5:40 a.m. his engine stopped as did the engines of the two other cars. When the drivers got out to see what was wrong they saw an egg-shaped spaceship wrapped in a blue haze on the beach. Kehoe claimed two "little men" (about 5 feet 5 inches,) got out of the object and asked questions of him and the two other drivers, such as: 'Where we were going? Who we were? What time it was? etc.' He said their skin appeared to be yellowish-green in the early morning light, but that otherwise they looked normal. He said they were wearing black leather pants, white belts, and light-colored jerseys.

USAF personnel spotted six saucer shaped flying objects' at an altitude of about 7000 feet at the base of a cloud bank about 3:50 PM; according to the Los Angeles Times Nov. 6, 1957.

The two other drivers were identified as Ronald Burke of Redondo Beach and Joe Thomas of Torrance, and Kehoe claimed Thomas called the police. He said they sounded as though they were talking English but he couldn't understand them, and said simply that he had to go to work. The men got back into their ship and disappeared into the sky, whereupon his car started up immediately. The ship was oval, tan or cream in color, with two metal rings around it upon which the object apparently rested, according to Kehoe.

Much of this story is recorded in, "Encounters with UFO Occupants", by Jim and Coral Lorenzen, 1976. The book is now out of print, but claims the incident was covered up by the U.S. Government.

There are also regular 2AM sightings of little green men, Easter bunnies, gnomes and faeries, reported by local residents leaving Playa Del Rey Bars, such as the Shack and the Prince of Whales; but you can take it or leave that.

Forty-two

The Great 1973 High School Senior Graduation Prank-Playa Del Rey, CA

1973 High School graduates had roll model/President Richard Nixon to look up to.

1973 was actually a tumultuous time in the World, but being at a small Catholic school in Playa Del Rey, most of it passed us by. Vietnam was on the mind of every 17 and 18 year old, however. We knew we were goners.

The Godfather took best Oscar, Miami won the Super bowl, and Secretariat the Kentucky Derby (and later the Triple Crown). I think Skylab was launched about then. Lyndon Johnson died in January, and they declared it a school holiday; a practice that schools has stopped: closing for the death of a President.

Most of just counted time, until it was time for us to go to Vietnam; but when President Nixon suspended the draft, we suddenly had to start making plans.

There was a great spring swell that year, and the water was well above normal temperatures, and we all surfed whenever we could. The waves were simply amazing, and those warm spring days rolled right into summer for most of us.

However, our class: the best class that ever went through that high school was forbidden a high school tradition: our senior ditch day. How could they do this to us? What had we done to deserve this?

These were some of the last good days of our adolescent lives; without much responsibility, and with a new, albeit unsure, future, we knew we had to rage against the machine.

The St. Bernard High School Campus, Playa Del Rey, CA.

So with that renewed determination, we began to hold secret planning sessions, as if we were actors from the movie, *The Great Escape*. We considered all aspects of the plan; security, labor, organization and optimum dates. In the end, we announced to our small group of conspirators that we would launch the plan on Sunday night, May 27, 1973; a near moonless night. They would pay for this!

We called it: "Operation: Tom, Duck and Harry."

Operation Tom; would upset the inside of the campus, Operation Duck; upset the school building, and Operation Harry; upset the perimeter of the campus.

The plan was simple really. After our parents went to bed, we would all sneak out of our homes, and rendezvous near the Dale's Junior Market on Manchester Boulevard. About forty of us showed up. We made our way into the school yard, protected by two roving guards in cars with walkie-talkie's, who circled the surrounding streets and fed us intelligence.

Working from a pencil sketch, etched out by one of our brighter science students, we met in the center of the school yard, and began to erect a three-story pyramid, made from the very heavy school benches used for lunch hour; Operation Tom.

Meanwhile, at Del Rey Lagoon, my good friend Mike Moffett headed to Del Rey Lagoon, and using gunny sacks, picked up a dozen or so ducks. We picked the locks of the school building, and let the ducks go in the hallways and re-locked the doors; Operation Duck.

Finally, thinking that way only young men do at age 17 and 18, fearless and sure of ourselves, we inserted blank keys into the padlocks of the school gates, and broke them off; Operation Harry.

Pleased with our operation, we all proceeded to our homes, slept an hour or so, and then rose again so that we could witness the devastation of Saint Bernard High School, by the graduation class of 1973.

The first time I knew that the operation had gone wrong, was when I approached the campus and to my surprise, there were no long lines of cars. We have never heard of bolt cutters, but the school's maintenance man had. As we headed to first period, we heard the sirens of the fire trucks, which our principal had called. Tension grew.

Finally, the area where the ducks were let loose was in shambles. We did not know then that a duck, when scared, tends to empty his bowels; and those ducks had just spent four five hours doing just that. Things were a mess; and I mean that literally.

The Great 1973 Tower.

It seemed so mighty to us, we were sure that astronauts could see it from space. We knew that this proud edifice; testimony to our solidarity against the school and the teachers that cost us our "Ditch Day," would stand for centuries.

The fire department used their hook and ladder to get to the top story of the benches, and then got some underclassman to remove the rest. By lunch hour, things were normal again.

We learned a lot that day; about ourselves and about working as a team and keeping things confidential. No classmate ever ratted on any other about the great senior prank of 1973, and we all somehow graduated in June.

Mostly we learned what a damn mess a few ducks can make.

DAVID DUKESHERER IS THE AUTHOR OF:

BEACH OF THE KING, THE EARLY HISTORY OF PLAYA DEL REY/WESTCHESTER/PLAYA VISTA, CALIFORNIA,
&

TOM LIEB-IN THE SHADOW OF KNUTE ROCKNE

CENTAL Historical Group, Inc.

Los Angeles, California USA

The Cental logo includes the Rancho La Ballona cattle brand

www.rancholaballona.com

Dedicated to preserving the memory of

Rancho's La Ballona and Aguaje Centinela

⊰CENTAL

Dedicated to preserving the memory of
Rancho's La Ballona & Aguaje Centinela

Made in the USA
Lexington, KY
22 September 2010